Crime, Punishment and Protest 1450 to the Present Day

STEPHEN LEE

General Editor: Josh Brooman

 LONGMAN

Introduction

Every society is protected by laws. Their purpose is to prevent some individuals from doing things which will harm others. If these laws are broken, a crime has been committed. Throughout the period covered by this book, crimes can be divided into three main types:

Table 1

Types of crime	
Crimes against the person	Murder, manslaughter, armed robbery, violence, sexual crimes like rape.
Crimes against property	Theft from shops, burglary, theft of horses and sheep, poaching, forgery, fraud, smuggling, piracy.
Crimes against authority	Treason, heresy, witchcraft, conspiracy.

Protest against authority was normally considered a crime before the twentieth century. More recently, however, some forms of protest have been permitted; people can express their views in writing or take part in a demonstration. These become crimes only if other people are hurt or property is damaged.

People commit crimes for many different reasons:

Table 2

Reasons for crime	
Need	Crime is caused by poverty or unemployment.
Belief	Crime is against the existing authority or religion through the belief that these are wrong and should be changed.
Impulse	Crime is committed on the spur of the moment.
Influences	Crime is committed under the influence of other people, or stimulants like alcohol or drugs.
Gain	Crime is carried out to acquire money or goods for profit.

A punishment is the penalty imposed by the authorities on a person who has been found guilty of a crime, by the process of law. This penalty usually involves some form of suffering. Why should the authorities want to do this? Different theories have been given for punishing criminals:

Table 3

Theories of punishment	
Retribution	Punishment gives the public the satisfaction that a criminal has been properly dealt with by the authorities. There may well be a feeling of revenge.
Deterrence	Punishment is intended to deter others from committing a similar crime.
Rehabilitation	Punishment reforms the criminal. It may also help him or her to become a law-abiding member of society again.
Restitution	Punishment makes the criminal provide some sort of compensation to the victim or to society. This may be part of the process of rehabilitation.
Removal	Punishment is intended to dispose of the criminal, either for a while or permanently. Society is to be protected from, or rid of, certain types of criminal.

There have always been disagreements about which of these is the most useful. The type of punishment also varies a great deal (see Table 4).

Table 4

Types of punishment

Capital punishment	Executions of various kinds, including beheading, hanging, and burning at the stake.
Mutilation	Cutting off parts of the body: for example, removal of ears or slitting nostrils.
Corporal punishment	Whipping or punishment in the pillory or stocks.
Imprisonment	Confinement in cells, either alone or with others; work might be involved.
Transportation	Forcible removal to a convict colony in North America or Australia.
Fines	Punishment by payment of money.

This book examines the changes in the crimes committed over the past five centuries, in the theories of punishment, and in the types of punishment imposed.

Questions

1 Refer to the types of crime in Table 1. List all the crimes in what you consider to be the order of seriousness.

2 Select one crime referred to in Table 1.
   a Look at the theories of punishment in Table 3 and list them in order of usefulness in dealing with the crime you have chosen. Give your reasons.
   b Look at the types of punishment in Table 4. List these in order of usefulness in dealing with the crime you have chosen. Give your reasons.

3 Look at Table 2. Would any of these reasons for crime change the answers you have given in question 2? Explain why.

4 Look at Sources 1 and 2. Both are about theories of punishment. Which theory does each illustrate? Give reasons for your choice.

Source 1

Old Testament (Exodus 21:24).

And if any mischief follow, then thou shalt give life for life, eye for eye, tooth for tooth.

Source 2

An eighteenth century judgement given by Mr Justice Buller, while sentencing a horse-thief to death.

You are to be hanged not for stealing horses, but that horses may not be stolen.

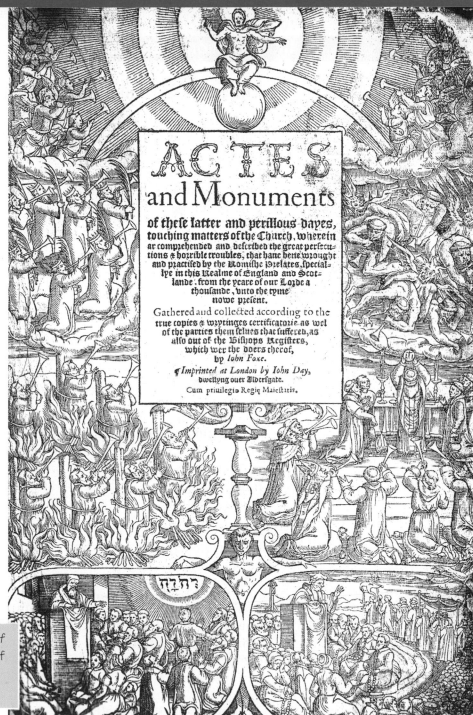

The opening page of Foxe's *Book of Martyrs*, written after the reign of Mary I to record the burning of Protestants.

Part 1 of this book covers the periods of the Tudors, the Stuarts and the early Hanoverians. Unit 1 deals with crimes against authority. In order of seriousness, these were treason, heresy, witchcraft and vagrancy. Unit 2 explores crimes against the person and against property, including violence, theft, poaching and smuggling. In both Units, the crimes and the punishments are looked at together.

Unit 1 · Crimes against authority

The most serious of all crimes

A rebellion was an attempt to overthrow a monarch or a government with the use of arms. Treason was a crime against the interests of the state. The two may, or may not, have been the same. If a rebellion failed, the rebels were found guilty of treason and condemned as traitors. If, on the other hand, it succeeded, then the government which had been overthrown might itself be considered treasonable.

Who rebelled and why?

The men and women involved in rebellions against their ruler would have had a variety of reasons. They must have believed in these very firmly, in view of the seriousness of their acts. They would have used one or more of the following arguments:

1 The monarch had usurped (falsely gained) powers which rightly belonged to another dynasty (royal line) or person. Henry Tudor believed this when he campaigned against Richard III in 1485; so did the Jacobites when they rebelled against George I in 1715 and against George II in 1745.

2 The monarch represented a false religion and so it was necessary in God's eyes to change the monarch in order to change the religion. Examples are Wyatt's rebellion against Mary I (1553–4), the Northern rebellion against Elizabeth I (1569), and the gunpowder plot against James I (1605).

3 The king or queen's government was not giving enough attention to the basic needs of the people, who therefore had to take matters into their own hands. Examples were the Pilgrimage of Grace (1536) during the reign of Henry VIII, and Kett's rebellion against Edward VI (1549).

4 The monarch had become a tyrant and was unwilling to share any powers with Parliament. As a result, Parliament had no alternative but to remove the monarch. There were two examples during the seventeenth century. The first revolution overthrew Charles I, while the second one removed James II in 1688 and placed William III and Mary on the throne.

Arguments against rebellion

Naturally, those who were in power put up the strongest case they could against rebellion. The Tudors were especially sensitive, since they had come to the throne through force against the Yorkists. Obviously they did not want to find themselves overthrown by another dynasty.

To the Tudor and Stuart monarchs, rebellion was the worst of all crimes. This was for two reasons:

1 They believed that the powers of the monarch came from God alone, by the Divine Right of Kings. Anyone taking part in a rebellion was therefore acting directly against God's will.

Source 1

The view of Richard Taverner, a writer and reformer in the sixteenth century.

Kings represent unto us the person even of God himself.

2 Society itself was a delicate system of masters and servants, all owing their loyalty to the king and to God. Breaking this system through rebellion was a terrible crime. It threatened a total upset in the kingdom, leading to civil war and destruction.

Source 2

The view of William Gouge, a Puritan writer in the seventeenth century.

They that are superiors to some are inferiors to others ... The master that hath servants under him, may be under the authority of a magistrate. Yea, God hath so disposed every one's several place, as there is not any one, but in some respect is under another, and all under the king. The king himself is under God.

Nowhere is the danger of rebellion pointed out more clearly than in the works of the playwright William Shakespeare, who wrote during the reigns of Elizabeth I and James I.

Punishment of treason

Since treason was considered the worst of all crimes, special attention was given to making the treatment of rebels as unpleasant as possible.

After their arrest, most suspects would be interrogated for a long time and would probably be tortured to find out the names of others involved in the plot. They would then be brought to trial. If found guilty of treason, they would almost certainly be executed.

There were two types of executions, depending on the social class of the condemned person. Aristocrats, who were usually wealthy people from the upper class, were likely to be beheaded with an axe, especially if they had royal blood. Depending on the skill of the executioner, death was normally immediate.

Source 3

An original illustration of the beheading of Mary Queen of Scots in 1587.

Commoners from lower classes, including priests, were likely to suffer the far worse fate of being hanged, drawn, and quartered. This punishment was introduced in the Middle Ages for treason. Edward I, a medieval king, had ordered its use against William Wallace in Scotland, as a punishment for rebellion. It was revived by the Tudors and Stuarts, and carried out mostly during the reigns of Elizabeth I, James I, and Charles II. It meant:

Source 4

A description of the grim punishment for traitors, from an 1800 Act of Parliament.

That the offender be dragged to the gallows; that he be hanged by the neck and then cut down alive; that his entrails be taken out and burned while he is yet alive; that his head be cut off; that his body be divided into four parts and that his head and quarters be at the King's disposal.

After his death, the traitor's lands and goods were taken by the monarch.

Source 5

A drawing, published in 1795, of the execution in 1605 of the gunpowder plotters against James I.

The significance of this horrible form of execution was explained by Lord Coke, a legal expert, in the eighteenth century:

Source 6

Lord Coke, *Institutes of the Laws of England*.

The reason is that his body, lands, goods, posterity, etc, should be torn, pulled asunder and destroyed, that intended to destroy the majesty of government.

He continued by giving a symbolic meaning for each stage of the traitor's death:

He was dragged to the scaffold because he was 'not worthy any more to tread upon the earth whereof he was made'.
He was hanged 'by the neck between heaven and earth, as deemed unworthy of both, or either'.
He was drawn because he 'inwardly had conceived and harboured in his parts such horrible treason'.
He was beheaded because here he had 'imagined the mischief'.

Death and social class

It seems unfair that there was such a huge difference in the type of execution given out for the same offence. Why was this?

It was due partly to a belief in the social order. Aristocrats or nobles were higher up the scale and therefore should not suffer a commoner's fate whatever their crime. Also, the monarch depended on some nobles to give information about the treasonable activities of others, whom they probably knew well. Would they have done this if they had known that their friends would be hanged, drawn and quartered?

Right or wrong?

The last person to be hanged, drawn and quartered was the Jacobite, Francis Towneley in 1746. But the punishment remained legal for a long time afterwards.

In 1813 there was a debate in Parliament, in which an M.P., Romilly, tried but failed to put an end to the punishment by law. He argued that it was a piece of barbarism from the Middle Ages and that it should not be used in more civilised times.

Against this, another M.P. said:

Source 7

The argument of M.P. Frankland against Romilly in 1813.

abolition To abolish a law means to do away with it.

> I do contend that the mere disuse of a law is no reason for its abolition. On the contrary, it may be the strongest reason for its continuance ... Because the sword of justice has not been used for a century, are we to destroy it? ... Because the edge has not for years been tried are we to blunt it?

Another point was raised in this debate. The death sentence was used for over 200 different crimes. How could treason be put across as the most serious of all unless it had its own particular form of execution?

Source 8

The view of the Solicitor-General, a government law officer, in 1813.

bulwark A safeguard or form of security.

> Ought a greater disgrace to be attached to the murder of the meanest subject than to the murder of a virtuous king? Are the safeguards, are the ancient landmarks, the bulwarks of the Constitution thus hastily to be removed?

Views like this meant that the punishment was not made illegal until 1870.

Questions

1 Using the ideas in this section, write down ideas for a debate about the statement: 'All rebellion between 1450 and 1750 was a crime'.

2 What was the main motive behind the punishments for treason: retribution, deterrence, rehabilitation, restitution, or removal? (Refer to Table 3 on page 3.) Place these in what you consider their order of importance.

3 Write a speech for Romilly to use in response to Frankland and the Solicitor-General. Then write responses to that speech.

1.2   Crimes of religion

In the Middle Ages, any departure from the beliefs of the Church had been tried in Church courts. During the sixteenth century, however, governments became more involved in religious matters. They made many religious changes during the reigns of Henry VIII, Edward VI, Mary I and Elizabeth I. The people had to observe these or face the consequences. What had once been a religious offence now became a crime against the state.

Precisely what form this crime took depended on who was in power at the time. This section compares the action taken against Protestants during the reign of Mary I with that taken against Catholics during the reign of Elizabeth I.

Source 1

Portrait of Mary Tudor (reigned 1553–58).

Were Protestants punished for the same reasons as Catholics?

Mary's punishment of Protestants

Mary Tudor was a devout Catholic who saw it as her duty before God to restore England to the Catholic Church. The religious changes introduced during the reigns of Henry VIII and Edward VI were all cancelled. Those of her subjects who refused to acknowledge the Pope as head of the Church in England were considered 'heretics' (people with contrary beliefs). She decided to concentrate her efforts on those who had led the changes to Protestantism. They were tried in front of Mary's most loyal supporter, Bishop Gardiner. They were offered a pardon if they recanted (renounced their views) but were sentenced to be burned at the stake if they did not.

Altogether, some 300 people suffered the fate of burning during Mary's reign. The most famous of these victims were the Bishops Hooper, Ridley, Latimer and Cranmer. Hooper was the first. His burning has been vividly described by a modern American historian:

Source 2

From W. Durant, *The Story of Civilisation 'The Reformation'*, (1957).

Usually a bag of gunpowder was placed between the legs of the condemned, so that the flames would cause a speedy death; but in Hooper's case the wood burned too slowly, the powder failed to explode, and the former bishop suffered agonies for almost an hour.

The details of the other burnings were carefully recorded in Foxe's *Acts and Monuments*, written after the end of Mary's reign. It is highly sympathetic to the victims, and critical of Mary herself, and for this reason it is usually called the *Book of Martyrs*.

Ridley and Latimer were burned on 6 October 1555. According to Foxe, they were chained to a post and gunpowder was tied to their neck in a bag. Cranmer was much affected by the agonies of Hooper's death. At first he gave up his former beliefs as 'heresies' and stated that he accepted all the doctrines of the Catholic Church. But Mary still decided that Cranmer should be executed. On the morning of his burning on 21 March 1556, he was supposed to complete his recantation in St Mary's Church in Oxford. But, to everyone's surprise, he concluded:

Source 3

An extract from Foxe's *Book of Martyrs*, first published in 1563.

setting abroad Publicising.

And now I come to the great thing, which so much troubleth my conscience more than anything that ever I did or said in my whole life, and that is the setting abroad of a writing contrary to the truth; which now here I renounce … as written for fear of death … And forasmuch as my hand offended, writing contrary to my heart, my hand shall first be punished therefor.

When he came to be burned, Cranmer stretched out the hand which had signed the recantation. He did this so 'that all men might see his hand burned before his body was touched'.

Mary was remembered as a tyrant and was nicknamed 'Bloody Mary'. This was because the *Book of Martyrs* influenced people's views for centuries.

Elizabeth's punishment of Catholics

Elizabeth I ended all Mary's attempts to return England to the Catholic Church. Instead, she re-introduced the measures of the English Reformation, including the Act of Supremacy, which made the monarch the head of the English Church. Catholic forms of worship now became illegal and Catholics themselves came under heavy suspicion.

Source 4

Illustration from Foxe's *Book of Martyrs*, showing the burning of Latimer and Ridley.

Source 5

Portrait of Elizabeth I (reigned 1558–1603).

During the reign of Elizabeth there was much Catholic activity in England. This was due partly to Cardinal William Allen (1532–94), who refused to take the Oath of Supremacy to Elizabeth and fled to Rome. In 1568 he set up a seminary in Douai in the Spanish Netherlands, to train priests. From Douai came a stream of Catholics who hoped to reconvert England. They knew what to expect: the walls in their refectory had pictures of executions and tortures preparing them, if necessary, for martyrdom. Altogether some 250 catholics were rounded up to be hanged, drawn, and quartered.

Source 6

The execution of Campion.

Some also became involved in the various plots against Elizabeth, which centred on the claims of Mary Queen of Scots to the throne. Others merely taught the Catholic faith. One of these was Edward Campion who preached throughout England. He was hunted down, imprisoned, tortured and finally executed on 1 December 1581.

There was little sympathy in books written in England for victims like Campion. On the other hand, books printed in Catholic countries in the rest of Europe likened the English Protestants to 'ravening wolves'. *De Persecutione Anglicana* ('English Persecution') was published in Rome in 1582; this dealt in as much detail with the fate of the Catholics under Elizabeth as Foxe's *Book of Martyrs* did with the sufferings of the Protestants under Mary.

Mary I and Elizabeth I compared

Mary I enforced the law of heresy against leading Protestants. The crime of these people was refusing to return to the Catholic Church and accept the supreme authority of the Pope. But did Elizabeth follow the same type of policy? Did she persecute Catholics because they were Catholics? One modern English historian writes:

Source 7

G.R. Elton, *England Under the Tudors*, (1955).

specious A specious argument is a false one.

Elizabeth always claimed that no one was persecuted in England for his religion: the trials of the Catholic priests were always for treason. It was a sound enough argument on the surface, but specious withal; for the priests did not in fact commit treason except inasmuch as they were priests.

Questions

1. Certain Protestants during Mary's reign were executed for 'heresy', some Catholics during Elizabeth's reign for 'treason'. Was there a difference?

2. How important is Foxe's *Book of Martyrs* as a source for the study of the treatment of heretics during this period?

3. Examine the illustration showing the execution of Latimer and Ridley (Source 4), and of Campion (Source 6). Both are English sources, but they serve different purposes. What are these?

4. Were 'martyrs' criminals?

1.3 Witchcraft

Why was witchcraft a crime?

During the Middle Ages witchcraft had, like heresy, been considered an offence against the Church, to be dealt with by Church courts. Even then, it had not been very common and the penalties for conviction had been light.

Then three Acts of Parliament were introduced in less than a hundred years. These tightened up the law and made witchcraft an offence against the state, and therefore a criminal act. The first was Henry VIII's Act of 1542, which imposed the death sentence for witchcraft. This was followed, during the reign of Mary, by the Act of 1563, which distinguished between major and minor forms of witchcraft. Major forms of witchcraft included seeking the death of a victim or attempting to raise spirits from the dead. The punishment for these was death. Minor forms of witchcraft involved other uses of magic; these were punishable by imprisonment or the stocks. Finally, James I's Act of 1604 brought together all earlier laws.

Witchcraft and the state

Why had the state suddenly become interested in witchcraft, after having left the Church to deal with it for so long? Several reasons can be given for this.

Like the rest of Europe in the sixteenth century, England went through the Reformation. This brought about huge changes in the way in which people worshipped. It also divided one religious group from another, so it became commonplace for Catholics and Protestants to call each other 'heretics' or 'antichrist'. Smaller forms of activity, like witchcraft, were drawn into this conflict and became the target of Catholics and Protestants alike.

The state introduced most of these religious changes. Henry VIII, for example, set up the Anglican Church and ordered the dissolution (break up) of the monasteries. Further changes took place under Edward VI before Mary I tried to make England Catholic again. Governments were so concerned about changing the main religious activities of the country, that it was impossible for them to ignore witchcraft, a growing practice in England.

In any case, the Tudors wanted to strengthen the power of the government after a long period of chaos when the Wars of the Roses had occurred. In doing this, they were determined to tighten up on *all* forms of activity against the power of the Crown. Witchcraft was considered a conspiracy because it involved a great deal of secrecy.

Witchcraft and the people

The people also became more concerned about witchcraft. This was partly because many faced uncertainty in their everyday lives. The rise in prices and the changing patterns of land use led to widespread poverty. Faced with difficult times ahead, many people became more and more superstitious. They either tried to make use of magic to improve their own lot, or they accused others of doing so. A major motive for accusing others might well have been envy. Certain individuals were, for example, targeted because of their success in growing crops or raising animals.

In times of uncertainty, especially in the period of civil war in the 1640s, unpleasant prejudices, which were usually kept quiet, became much more obvious. One of these was misogyny (hatred of women). Over 90 per cent of those accused of witchcraft in Essex were women, usually elderly and living alone. According to a writer of the 1690s:

Source 1

The view of William Perkins.

prevail To be present in, or triumph over.

> Woman being the weaker sex is sooner entangled by the devil's illusions with this damnable art than the man ... in all ages it is found true by experience that the devil hath more easily and oftener prevailed with women than with men.

Finally, some prominent people influenced the state to act against witchcraft. One was King James VI of Scotland (later also James I of England), who wrote:

Source 2

James I's book: *Demenologie* (1597).

> There are so many at this time and in this country of these detestable slaves of the Devil, the witches, that it has encouraged me to write this book ... so I can convince the doubting hearts of many, both that such assaults by Satan are practised and that the guilty should be punished.

How was witchcraft dealt with?

Searching out and punishing witches

In theory, capital punishment could be imposed for more serious cases of witchcraft. 'Evidence' was not difficult to find. Certain types of marks on the body would be enough, since these were supposed to be caused by witches feeding their 'familiar' (cats, toads, or birds) with their own blood. Alternatively, one witch might name another as part of a confession, or evidence might be provided by two witnesses of a witch having made a pact, or deal, with the Devil. Although torture was not permitted, the accused person could be deprived of sleep by interrogators for long periods. Sometimes, too, local crowds would take matters into their own hands and apply the old-fashioned 'swimming test'. The accused would be submerged in water, and if they rose to the surface they were assumed guilty.

Source 3

A sixteenth century print showing the 'swimming test' being applied to an accused woman.

The courts had the power to sentence to death by hanging but not, as many people think, by burning at the stake.

Although witchcraft was a criminal offence, the use of state powers against it varied enormously. One of the problems is that records were kept only for official trials. We know that between 1563 and 1700 about 2000 people were tried in assize courts (see page 25) and a further 1000 in Church courts. Of these, some 400 were hanged, although there is no way of finding out accurately how many more were killed by angry mobs.

Witchcraft and hysteria

The persecution of witches was not carried out evenly throughout the period. Instead, it seemed to go in waves. The first of these took place in the reigns of Mary and Elizabeth, followed by an easing-up during the reign of James I. The peak was reached later, during the 1640s, the period of the Civil War. At this time, the so-called 'Witchfinder General', Matthew Hopkins, hunted and punished witches in Norfolk, Suffolk, Ely, Cambridgeshire, Northamptonshire, Huntingdonshire and, above all, Essex.

Source 4

An illustration from a book by Matthew Hopkins, called *The Discovery of Witches*.

Hopkins operated with a team which included Mary Phillips, who searched for the 'witch's mark' on the bodies of the accused. He created widespread panic and terror in a population already terrified by the Civil War, and probably went much further than the authorities had originally intended. In Source 5, a modern historian offers an explanation of the reasons for Hopkins's ruthless campaign.

Source 5

A. Macfarlane, 'Witchcraft', a section in Purnell's *History of the English Speaking Peoples*.

zeal Enthusiasm, keenness.
benefactor A person who helps others.

At first, at least, he does not seem to have been motivated by desire for financial gain, nor was he at any time driven by religious zeal. He felt himself to be a public benefactor, dealing with a menace which soon astonished him by its huge proportions.

Unpleasant though some episodes were, the punishment of witchcraft in England and Wales was far less extreme than in the rest of Europe, or even in Scotland. An American historian writes:

Source 6

G. Salgado, *The Elizabethan Underworld*, (1984).

It must be noted that as far as England is concerned, there is no evidence to suggest the existence of anything like an organised witch cult with covens, black sabbaths, midnight orgies and aerial transportation ... What we do find are lonely old women living on the edge of poverty ... often their only companions were a pet cat, a toad, or a weasel.

The numbers of trials and executions were also much lower in England and Wales than elsewhere, and there were no burnings at the stake. By contrast, Como in northern Italy had 1000 burnings in a single year. The scene of a burning must have been even more terrible than that of a hanging.

The end of witchcraft as a crime

The last time anyone was executed for witchcraft was in 1682. The last witchcraft trial took place in 1712, and the various laws about witchcraft were abolished in 1736. Mainly responsible for this decline was a gradual change in attitudes. During the late sixteenth and early seventeenth centuries, religious differences became less important as more reasonable and secular (non-religious) influences began to take hold. What had once been seen as witchcraft and magic could now be explained as natural. Books were now written *against* witchcraft trials and even against the previously-accepted notions of hell and the devil.

On the other hand, it took time for such changes to affect the whole of society. People reacted in different ways to the growth of rational views. Better educated people were more likely to accept them, although some individuals might have had their own motives for continuing to believe in witches and witchcraft. In the rural areas, by contrast, whole communities lived with prejudices which had become deeply rooted because they were related to social customs.

Much to their surprise, the witch-hunters, still convinced they were doing the right thing, now found themselves accused of criminal behaviour.

Source 7

J.A. Sharpe, *Early Modern England*, (1987).

In 1751 Ruth Osborne, a suspected witch, was subjected to the swimming test at Tring, Hertfordshire, and died after the experience. Thomas Colley, a local chimney-sweep who had played a part in the swimming, was later hanged for her murder, a neat demonstration of how the attitudes of the courts had changed.

Questions

1 Look again at the reasons given in this section for the growth of state action against witchcraft.
   a Divide the reasons into political, social, economic, religious and personal influences.
   b Give an example of the way one reason might have led to another.
   c Give an example of one reason which might have been the result of another reason.
   d Can any of the reasons be considered more important than the others? Explain your answer.

2 Explain why people might have supported and opposed the persecution of witches
   a during the 1640s
   b after 1700.

3 Do the sources in this section suggest the view that the treatment of witchcraft in England was
   a widespread
   b harsh?

4 Which of the sources in this section have you found
   a most reliable
   b most useful?
   Explain your answers.

1.4 Vagrancy

During the sixteenth and seventeenth centuries huge numbers of vagrants, or wanderers, roamed through the countryside and loitered in the villages and towns. Usually they were alone or in family groups, but often they were seen in larger bands. Since they were considered to be a real threat to the rest of the community, they were soon regarded as criminals and were therefore subject to criminal law.

Who were they? A whole new vocabulary emerged to describe them. Men were normally called 'rogues'. Some of these might be 'dummerers', who were genuine or pretended mutes (people who could not speak), while many would also be 'palliards', or beggars. Rogues were often able to produce forged identity papers. They might also pose as 'upright' men, appearing to be well-dressed and respectable.

They were sometimes accompanied by their womenfolk, or 'doxies' and even by their children. Boys were called 'kinchin coes' and girls 'kinchin mortts'. Some had been deliberately mutilated by their parents so that they would attract the pity of passers-by and therefore be more successful beggars.

Why did vagrancy exist?

The reasons for vagrancy across the countryside need careful explanation. Some may be seen as *objective*, or entirely beyond the control of the vagrants. Others may be considered *subjective*, or their own fault. As you

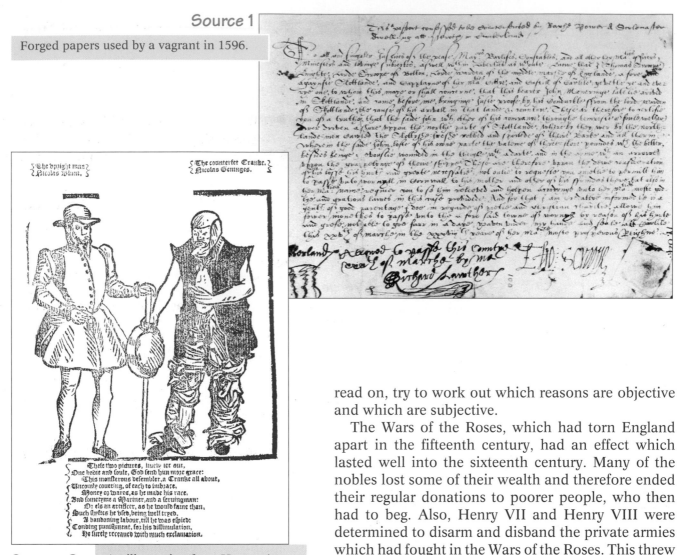

Source 1

Forged papers used by a vagrant in 1596.

Source 2

An illustration from Harman's *Caveat* (1566), warning against rogues posing as 'upright men'.

read on, try to work out which reasons are objective and which are subjective.

The Wars of the Roses, which had torn England apart in the fifteenth century, had an effect which lasted well into the sixteenth century. Many of the nobles lost some of their wealth and therefore ended their regular donations to poorer people, who then had to beg. Also, Henry VII and Henry VIII were determined to disarm and disband the private armies which had fought in the Wars of the Roses. This threw large numbers of ex-soldiers into poverty. There was great disruption:

Source 3

A late fifteenth century ballad: a poem set to music.

> Temporal lords be almost gone,
> Households keep they few or none,
> Which causeth many a goodly man
> For to beg his bread:
> If he steal for necessity,
> There is none other remedy …

temporal lords Nobles or aristocrats.

Matters were made worse during the reign of Henry VIII by the dissolution of the monasteries. This had a double effect: it removed a regular source of help for the poor, and also deprived many monastery suppliers of their livelihood. Butchers, launderers, cooks and gardeners suddenly found themselves out of business.

More important still was an economic revolution which was taking place in parts of England and Wales in Tudor times. Wealthy merchants were buying up large amounts of land, for which they then charged higher rents. Alternatively, the merchants changed the use of land from crop farming into sheep pasture. The change was noticed as early as 1516:

Source 4

Sir Thomas More's *Utopia*, (1516).

> Your sheep that were wont to be so meek and tame, and so small eaters, now, as I hear say, be become so great devourers and so wild, that they eat up, and swallow down the very men themselves. They consume, destroy, and devour whole fields, houses and cities.

To add to this was the rapid inflation of the 1540s and 1550s. The value of money fell in the 1540s and the purchasing power of wages fell during the sixteenth century by at least 60 per cent. The result was poverty and an increase in crime.

Source 5

The view of Robert Crowley, in 1549.

yoke Influence or domination.
chastisement Punishment.
garnished gallow-trees A reference to hanging.

> What honest householders have been made followers of other not so honest men's tables! ... What forward and stubborn children have hereby shaken off the yoke of godly chastisement, running headlong into all kinds of wickedness, and finally garnished gallow-trees!

Many people in Tudor and Stuart England assumed that the direct cause of vagrancy was idleness.

Source 6

The views of Edward Hext, a Somerset man, (1596).

> Work they will not, neither can they, without extreme pains, by reason their sinews are so benumbed and stiff through idleness, as their limbs being put to any hard labour will grief them beyond measure: so as they will rather hazard their lives than work.

The reason for idleness, it was often felt, was a serious fault in a person's character, which would be made even worse by drink.

Source 7

A print showing vagrants at an inn.

There were also strong written attacks on vagrants.

Source 8

Samuel Rid, *Martin Mark-all*, (1610).

> Loyterers laze in the streete, lurke in the Ale-houses, and range in the high-waies.

How were vagrants dealt with?

Punishments for vagrancy

The authorities believed that there was plenty of work available for those who wanted it. Those who did not should be punished for idleness. In 1572 an Act stated that vagrants could be:

Source 9

Act of Parliament in 1572.

> Grievously whipped, and burnt through the gristle of the right ear with a hot iron of the compass of an inch about.

In 1598 the law stated that:

Source 10

Act of Parliament in 1598.

> Every person found begging is to be stripped naked from the middle upwards, and openly whipped, until his or her body be bloody, and then passed to his or her birthplace or last place of residence, and in case they know neither, they are to be sent to the House of Correction for a year, unless someone gives them employment sooner.

Part of this can be seen being carried out in Source 11.

Source 11

The punishment of a vagrant as shown in a sixteenth century print.

Did these punishments work?

There is plenty of evidence that such measures only made the problem worse. The laws could not be properly enforced, because there were not enough officers. Furthermore, the more savage the punishment, the more organised crime became among vagrants. The assumption of the authorities of the time was that crime and vagrancy were one and the same. In fact, the measures they took helped toughen the criminals among the vagrants. Organised gangs grew up to improve methods of theft and burglary and to make arrest more difficult. Some vagrants went even further, moving beyond a life of petty crime in the towns to one as a highwayman on the main roads.

Other points of view

Not all the poor were treated as criminals. Tudor authorities tried to distinguish between those who were able-bodied but 'idle' and those who were unable to work through physical disability. An Act of 1563 gave Justices of the Peace the power to organise donations for the relief of these 'impotent poor', and in 1598 a poor-rate, or local tax, was introduced in each parish.

However, these measures did not work well. Instead, the authorities preferred to set up special institutions where the different types of poor people could be dealt with together. The most famous of the institutions was Bridewell hospital and house of correction, founded by Edward VI in 1553. Nicholas Ridley, Bishop of London, urged the government to use Bridewell, an empty palace to 'lodge Christ in':

Source 12

Nicholas Ridley writing to Sir William Cecil in January 1552.

The matter is, sir, alas! he [Christ] hath lain too long abroad without lodging in the streets of London, both hungry and naked and cold ... Sir, there is a wide, large, empty house of the King's Majesty's, called Bridewell, that would wonderfully well serve to lodge Christ in, if he might find such good friends in the court to procure his cause.

The citizens of London added their voice for the use of Bridewell.

Source 13

Petition from the citizens of London to the Privy Council.

And we considered also that the greatest number of beggars fallen into misery by lewd and evil service, by wars, by sickness, or other adverse fortune, have so utterly lost their credit, that though they would show themselves willing to labour, yet are they so suspected and feared of all men, that few or none dare, or will receive them to work.

The institution housed children and 'impotent poor' adults who could perform light work. But it also contained the 'sturdy' poor, who were first to be whipped. From the start, therefore, Bridewell was as much a place of correction and punishment as of charity. The idea spread to other parts of the country, including Exeter and Ipswich. The 1572 Poor Law gave counties the power to build houses of correction, and in the following years many were set up across the country. On arrival all adults were whipped and then shackled (bound in metal rings), a punishment which would be repeated often in the future.

Finally, the Great Poor Law was introduced in 1601 to bring together earlier measures of poor relief. Local councils collected a 'poor rate' to provide workhouses and hospitals. The system remained in existence for over two centuries.

Questions

1 Which of the reasons given for the increase in the number of vagrants would you consider *objective* (beyond their control) and which would you consider *subjective* (their own fault)? How do they connect to each other?

2 Using the information in this section, explain at what stage you think a poor person became a criminal.

3 Do the sources in this section show that at the time all people thought that all vagrants were criminals? How would you explain any differences in the views shown?

Unit 2 · Crimes against property and the person

2.1 Crimes against the person

What types of crime?

Crimes are said to be against the *person* if a person is the target. If, however, the criminal's target is the person's possessions rather than the person, a crime has been committed against *property*. Where the two overlap, the criminal's motive decides how the crime should be classified; this means, for example, that robbery counts as a crime against property. Numbers show that crimes against the person have always been fewer than crimes against property. This was certainly the case in the sixteenth and seventeenth centuries:

Source 1

Indictments (charges) for crime, 1550–1625.

Crimes	Middlesex	Sussex	Hertfordshire
Against persons	6%	11%	6%
Against property	93%	74%	86%

During this period, crimes against the person almost always involved some form of physical violence, leading either to death or 'actual bodily harm'.

Homicide

Homicide, or the act of killing another human being, has always been classified into either murder or manslaughter. An early definition of murder was provided by the legal expert, Blackstone, who believed that it occurred:

Source 2

Blackstone's *Commentaries*, volume 4.

When a person of sound memory and discretion unlawfully killeth a reasonable creature.

The crucial factors in defining murder then, as now, were whether it was intended beforehand, and the evil desire to do harm. Manslaughter, by contrast, was defined as killing which took place in the heat of the moment and was not therefore planned in advance.

Today the difference between murder and manslaughter is decided before the case actually comes to court and the charge is normally one or the other. During the period we are studying, however, the accused person was nearly always charged with murder, and the decision was made at the end of the trial by the jury. The accused would therefore be found guilty (of murder), or guilty of manslaughter, or not guilty.

Some recognition was given to special circumstances, such as insanity. In 1688 Elizabeth Waterman was acquitted (set free) by a Surrey jury:

Source 3

An extract from the Surrey court records.

The prisoner of the Barr being distracted and not of sound mind did kill Mary Waterman, her daughter, with a razor and that she came to her death by no other means.

Where a parent punished a child so severely that the child died, the accused parent was found guilty only if excessive violence had been used. In Tudor and Stuart times heavy beatings were considered quite normal and many parents were acquitted of murder.

In every part of England fewer women were involved in killing than men. Several reasons are suggested by a modern American legal historian.

Source 4

J.M. Beattie, *Crime and the Courts in England 1660–1800*, (1986).

Men were much more likely than women to be in taverns, to drink too much, to think their courage slighted, and to feel compelled to give and accept challenges to fight. They were also more likely to be carrying weapons or a knife or a tool of some kind.

Surprisingly, the proportion of the population found guilty of homicide (murder or manslaughter) gradually went down. The following table gives the example of Surrey.

Source 5

Convictions for homicide in Surrey, 1660–1802.

	Number found guilty of homicide	Rate per 100,000 population
1660–1679	21	2.5
1680–1699	23	1.5
1700–1719	16	2.1
1720–1739	12	0.9
1740–1759	33	1.4
1760–1779	26	0.7
1780–1802	18	0.3

Did this mean that people were becoming less violent? It would have taken a great deal to make this happen. Throughout the period people lived with violence at every level of their experience. Violence in the form of terror was applied by the state for many offences, and in full public view. Families experienced violence at home, where wives and children could be savagely beaten. There was frequent violence between men: duelling was common among the aristocracy, boxing or brawling among the lower social classes. Even recreation involved violence, and there were numerous cruel sports like cockfighting and bear baiting.

On the other hand, some historians have argued that things were beginning to improve by the end of the eighteenth century. The Methodists formed a religious body which broke away from the Church of England and concerned itself with social issues. This had a widespread influence on English society, and the family was considered more important, partly because of the personal example set by George III, who had a happy and stable marriage. There was therefore a greater social stability, although we cannot be sure about how far down through society this actually penetrated.

An alternative explanation for Source 5 is that the authorities were faced with a growing population and were therefore making fewer arrests per hundred thousand people. In other words, there was a better chance literally of getting away with murder by the eighteenth century.

Infanticide

A distinction was normally made between homicide and infanticide, the killing of an infant. Infanticide was treated in two different ways, which said a great deal about moral attitudes at the time.

If a married woman was accused of killing an infant, it would need to be proved in court that the baby had been born alive and that murder had been committed. Otherwise, she would have to be acquitted. She was, in other words, innocent unless proved guilty. Quite the reverse applied to unmarried women. Under an Act of 1624, they were assumed guilty unless they could prove their innocence. Even in cases where an unmarried woman kept secret the death of a stillborn baby, an offence was committed for which she could be hanged.

Such double standards were justified in 1680 as an attempt to reduce immorality. The 1624 Act was directed against:

Source 6

Zacharay Babington's *Advice to Grand Jurors*, (1680).

> Lewd whores, who having committed one sin, to avoid the shame, and the charge of a bastard ... privately destroy the infant.

lewd whores Prostitutes considered shameful.

This was a terrible injustice. Most unmarried mothers were not 'lewd whores' but unfortunate servants who had given birth alone and in squalid circumstances. They had managed to hide their pregnancy and now dared not report the stillbirth. They became the victims of an infanticide 'craze' during the seventeenth century, which led to more hangings than the more famous witch hunts.

During the eighteenth century treatment became fairer. More of an effort was made in all cases to find out whether the infant *had* been stillborn. The lungs were removed and put in a pail of water. If they sank it was assumed that they had never drawn breath. So in this way the law for unmarried women came to be the same as that for married.

Rape

Rape was as serious a problem in early modern England as in any other period. It is, however, difficult to get a true indication of its extent. Many cases went unreported because of the fear of embarrassment in court or pressure from the accused man. Authorities were often reluctant to press charges and juries frequently failed to convict.

During the eighteenth century there was a significant increase in the number of charges for rape. This could, however, indicate a change in attitudes. Now there were more charges brought against men, since women were more likely to be seen as unfortunate victims rather than temptresses as had often been thought in the seventeenth century.

Trials

If arrested for committing a crime, men and women could be brought before one of the following courts:

1 A magistrate's court, intended for the less serious offences. Magistrates might sit alone or in pairs during 'petty sessions'. They were prominent members of the community. Their jurisdiction was 'summary', meaning they had no jury to decide whether the accused was guilty.

2 A court of quarter sessions, which contained a larger number of magistrates and met four times a year in the counties and larger towns.

3 An assize court, which tried the most serious cases. They met twice a year in the leading county town. London's Old Bailey had eight sessions a year. These were headed by fully qualified judges, and the jury system was used.

Source 7

A trial at an assize court during the eighteenth century.

At any of these courts, first-time offenders were sometimes allowed to claim 'benefit of clergy'. This had originally been an appeal for mercy by members of the clergy (priests), on the grounds that they should have been tried by a Church court. Until the eighteenth century, benefit of clergy was being applied to anyone who could show literacy by reading an extract from the Bible. If successful, the person who had claimed benefit might be acquitted even after being found guilty.

Source 8

An original drawing of a hanging in the seventeenth century.

Punishments for crimes against the person

Those who had been found guilty and had not been successful in claiming benefit of clergy faced the prospect of harsh punishment.

The death sentence was applied to anyone convicted of murder and rape, and to unmarried mothers found guilty of infanticide or concealing a stillbirth. In most cases death was by hanging.

The one exception was that a woman convicted of murdering her husband would be burned at the stake. This was the punishment for a special crime known as 'petty treason', which was considered one of the very worst a woman could commit. Since a husband was considered a natural master, his murder was:

Source 9

Sir James Ansty, *General Charge to all Grand Juries*, (1725).

Against a Subject, between whom and the Offender, the Law presumes there is a special Obedience and Subjection.

During the eighteenth century the process was a little more merciful, as the hangman would try to strangle the condemned woman before the flames could take hold.

Source 10

A twentieth century drawing of a pillory in Elizabethan times.

Those acquitted of murder and found guilty of manslaughter were often branded on the hand and released. Alternatively, they might be whipped through the streets, as described on page 72. Apart from hanging, one of the most feared punishments was the 'pillory', a frame with holes for the criminal's head and hands. This might be accompanied by mutilation, like the removal of an ear. In the case of a sexual offender, there might also be attacks by an angry crowd.

Questions

1   Conduct a trial scene in class, based on the information given in this section. Include the charge, evidence, verdict, sentence, and appeal for 'benefit of clergy'.

2   'Justice gave women a worse deal than men'. Does the material in this section prove this?

3   Place the sources in this section in order of
a usefulness
b reliability.
Explain your choice.

2.2 Theft and robbery

This section concentrates on crimes against property carried out within and on the outskirts of the main towns, especially London.

Reasons for theft and robbery

People committed these crimes under two types of influence. One was external, where they were affected by conditions beyond their control. The other was internal, where crimes were the result of personal decisions. Most people were affected by both, although in different combinations.

External influences

These included rising food prices. There was often a close connection between increased wheat prices and levels of theft. People's lives were subject to widespread changes because most of their money went on food. Many were near the 'breadline', only just able to afford food, and bad conditions might drive them below it. There were also periods of recession, which resulted in unemployment and an increased threat of starvation. Those who were in employment might be underpaid and therefore tempted to steal to add to their wages.

Internal influences

These varied widely. In some cases theft became a habit, even a way of life. Some people justified it as a protest against the social and economic system. For others the motive was greed: the desire to have more and more possessions.

Most people committed their first crime as a spontaneous act. Those who re-offended were, however, likely to be drawn into a criminal network. There was a huge underworld of crime in London throughout the Tudor, Stuart and Hanoverian periods. London was especially attractive to criminal gangs. It was compact, had many wealthy residents, and there were many places to hide in and pass on stolen property.

Theft

Theft was by far the most common form of crime committed in all the cities and towns. It took various forms.

Shoplifting involved the stealing of goods from a shop or market stall. It grew as more and more goods were displayed. The theft of any item worth more than one shilling qualified for the death sentence.

Picking pockets was even more frequent, involving 'cutting' or removing purses and disappearing round the nearest corner (think of the phrase 'cut and run'). There were numerous gangs and 'schools' for young pickpockets.

Source 1

A report sent to Lord Burghley, chief minister during the reign of Elizabeth I.

One Wotton, a gentilman borne procured all the cutpurses about this cittie to repair to his said howse. There was a schole howse sett upp to learne younge boyes to cutt purses.

Again, picking pockets could lead to the death sentence. However, it was not often prosecuted because of the difficulty of making an arrest.

More effort was made to bring burglars and housebreakers to justice. Here are two descriptions of housebreaking in Elizabethan Essex. The first involves some valuable household objects.

Source 2

F.G. Emmison, *Elizabethan Life: Disorder*, details taken from Essex sessions and assize records.

s. Shilling, or five pence.

> On 30 September 1579 the house of the Earl of Sussex at Boreham (New Hall) was broken into by John Crosfield ... He removed a gilt bowl (worth £4), a silver bowl (30s.), a silver combcase (£4), and two silver trencher plates (30s.). Found guilty, he was hanged.

The second description concerns a small amount of cash.

Source 3

F.G. Emmison, *Elizabethan Life: Disorder*, details taken from Essex sessions and assize records.

d. An old sign for 'pence'.

> In 1597 Thomas Clarke, a great Bardfield husbandman, was sent to the gallows for burglary involving only 12d. [5p] in money.

Other cases resulted in fines or no punishment at all for similar offences; there were therefore big differences in the treatment of burglars. Much burglary was committed by carefully organised armed gangs. Valuable objects would often be sent abroad, especially to Holland because of its wide commercial networks.

The career of Jonathan Wild

One of the most influential criminals of this entire period was Jonathan Wild, who lived between 1685 and 1725.

His early life was spent as a bucklemaker's apprentice. He then drifted to London in 1709, where he was imprisoned for theft. The first year was spent in a dungeon called the Hole. It was:

Source 4

A description of 'the Hole' by the historian D. Rumbelow, in *I Spy Blue*, (1971).

> An underground cellar forty two feet long by fifteen feet wide and twelve feet high, without heat or light, the prisoners only telling if it was night or day by the light or lack of it shining down the chimney flue. There was little ventilation and no sanitation for the seventy men, women and children that existed there on scraps of food flung through the grating and so vile were the conditions that apothecaries refused to descend into 'the Hole' for even a few minutes.

He managed to gain the confidence of prison guards and was made a 'trusty'. After his release in 1712, he lived with a prostitute and pickpocket, Mary Milliner. She would lure the victims into an alley and he would strike and rob them. But Wild had greater ambitions than this.

He gradually became a leading light in London's underworld and was soon responsible for a large number of the thefts and burglaries in the capital. His safety rested on a simple policy. The law stated that anyone prosecuted for receiving stolen goods actually had to have them in his or her possession. Wild therefore made sure that he never did. He set up crimes and negotiated between the thief and the receiver of the goods.

Wild built up a network of over 7,000 thieves, whom he blackmailed into continuing to work for him. He often turned in some of the unreliable or weaker ones as a punishment, and was sometimes able to collect a

Source 5

Jonathan Wild, 'Thieftaker General'.

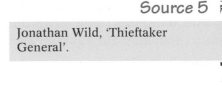

reward offered under an Act of 1692. He claimed that he was responsible for the hanging of 67 victims, although the actual number could be well over 200. For this reason he was often known as the 'Thieftaker General'.

He often went ahead of the cart carrying the condemned men to the gallows, announcing to the crowd that his 'children' were coming.

He became so famous that the government even passed an Act in 1717 (known as Jonathan Wild's Act) to stop his activities. But even then he was not arrested. Why not? According to a modern historian:

Source 6

J.J. Tobias, *Crime and Industrial Society in the 19th century,* (1967).

It is said that officers of the law were content to let him continue to operate because of the assistance he could give them ... Perhaps a more important reason was the efficiency with which he compromised all those who seemed likely to be dangerous, and the fear of giving evidence against him which he thus engendered.

Wild was eventually arrested in 1725 for helping a highwayman escape. Once he was safely in Newgate awaiting trial, witnesses came forward in their droves to give an account of his criminal activities. He was convicted and hanged at Tyburn.

Source 7

A woodcut of the end of Jonathan Wild.

Robbery

Robbery was very common in the seventeenth and eighteenth centuries, especially in city streets or on the roads approaching London. Most robbers had no horse, and were known as 'footpads'. Those on horseback were called 'highwaymen'. Footpads were more likely to be part of a gang, while most highwaymen worked alone or in small groups. The number of highwaymen increased during the first half of the eighteenth century. This was because the number of roads was greatly increased, and stagecoach services for passengers spread throughout the country.

Highwaymen were known to behave with elaborate courtesy. One example was James Maclean, known as the 'gentleman highwayman'. He described how he entered his occupation:

Source 8

Part of James Maclean's letter to *The Public Advertiser*, 29 February 1764.

I cannot reproach myself with doing any Thing unbecoming a Gentleman. When the scanty Allowance of five Hundred a Year that I had from that Old Gripe my Father was gone, having always entertain'd a just Contempt for the Pedantry of Study, and being above any mechanic Employment, I embraced the only Scheme left for a Man of Spirit, and commenced a *Gentleman of the Shade*, in which Occupation I have acquitted myself with equal Courage, Honour and Genius.

There was also a belief that highwaymen were more careful about robbing the poor. Maclean said that he had:

Source 9

Another part of James Maclean's letter to *The Public Advertiser*, 29 February 1764.

Obliged a couple of sneaking footpads to refund the week's wages they had taken from a poor labourer.

A modern legal historian offers the following explanation for this type of behaviour:

Source 10

J.M. Beattie, *Crime and the Courts in England 1660–1800*, (1986).

brace Pair.

Highwaymen, well mounted and armed with a brace of pistols, did not normally find it necessary to relieve such victims of their pennies. They were after larger gain: the coaches of the rich, farmers returning from market, or stagecoaches and the mail service.

Highwaymen were seen by the authorities as the most serious criminal threat of all. They threatened the very lifeline between towns, and regularly threatened the postal service. Large rewards were therefore offered for information, and any highwayman found guilty in court was usually hanged.

The career of Dick Turpin

Dick Turpin, highwayman, shoots Tom King in trying to save him from arrest.

Source 11

The most famous of all highwaymen was Dick Turpin. Born in Essex, he became a butcher's apprentice and married a local woman. But he was dissatisfied with a life of relative poverty. He drifted into a career of crime which started with sheep and horse theft and led on to smuggling activities along the Essex coast. Wanted by the authorities, he moved out of Essex. He turned to armed robbery in Lincolnshire and Yorkshire, before eventually being caught and hanged in York in 1739, ironically on charges of horse theft.

Turpin was far more isolated and less involved in organised crime than Jonathan Wild. He has been the subject of many legends, partly the result of a book called *Rookwood*, published in 1834 by Harrison Ainsworth. Many of his alleged exploits were imaginary, including a famous ride he is supposed to have made to York.

Questions

1 'Crime does not pay'. Does this apply to Jonathan Wild or Dick Turpin?

2 'Criminals made by their circumstances'. Is this a reasonable description of how Wild, Turpin and Maclean turned to crime?

3 What do the careers of Wild and Turpin show about the different ways in which crime was organised in the early eighteenth century?

4 Is it surprising that Wild and Turpin were eventually hanged on such minor charges?

5 Which of the two was:
a the more successful
b the more interesting?
Give reasons for your answers.

2.3   Rural crimes

What types of crime?

We have examined theft and robbery in towns. These crimes also, of course, took place in the countryside. The three offences most strongly associated with rural areas, however, were trespass, horse theft, and poaching.

Trespass
According to an eighteenth century legal expert:

Source 1

Blackstone, *Commentaries on the Laws of England*, (1768).

It signifies no more than entry on another man's ground without a lawful authority, and doing some damage, however inconsiderable.

This took a wide variety of forms. It might mean damage to fencing, hedges or crops. It was normally punishable by a fine, unless poaching or theft could be proved. Those accused of trespass would argue that they were carrying out an earlier right to 'glean' (collect the remnants of any crop after harvesting) or gather firewood. This view was strongly contested by the estate owners, who said that any earlier rights had disappeared when the land had been enclosed.

Horse theft
The theft of horses was a serious offence, for which capital punishment could be used. This was probably because horses were highly valued. Before the railways they provided the fastest form of transport and therefore the main form of mobility.

Horse theft normally went hand-in-hand with other crimes. Highwaymen, for example, nearly always stole the animals they rode and, indeed, Dick Turpin was hanged for horse theft.

Poaching

There were many parks all over the country which looked after game for use by the owners. Gamekeepers were employed to keep watch over them day and night. This was to try to prevent poaching, the most widespread crime in rural areas. Poaching meant illegal hunting or trapping of deer, hares, pigeons, pheasants, partridges, ducks, swans, hawks, and fish. Poachers used crossbows, fowling pieces (guns for shooting birds), dogs, nets over holes, or traps.

Poaching was forbidden by a confusing number of contradictory laws, dating back to the fourteenth century. Often a new law would be made without the previous one being cancelled. Blackstone, for example, stated that the game laws were:

Source 2

A poacher in action.

Source 3

Blackstone, *Commentaries on the Laws of England*, (1768).

> A variety of Acts of Parliament, which are so numerous and so confused, and the crime itself so questionable a nature ... the statutes for preserving the game are many and various and not a little obscure and intricate.

statute Written law.

The first law had been passed in 1389, but the best documented was the 1671 Game Act. This made it illegal for anyone to take game unless he had a freehold property worth £100 a year, or had a 99-year leasehold property worth £150 a year, or was the son and heir of a large property owner. This meant that some people could hunt anywhere they wished, while most were prevented from taking game even from their own property.

Why poach?

Why should anyone want to break these laws? Some poachers claimed to be different from the common thief because they felt that the laws of the land were unjust and that they had a natural right to hunt. There were also gangs of poachers who hunted entirely for profit. They were supplying food not for themselves but for the black market. During the reign of James I it became illegal to trade in game. People who did not have their own game parks had to poach or to find game on the growing black market. An Act of 1707 made the penalty for buying, selling or possessing game either a fine or imprisonment, but this did not work well.

Aristocracy against poachers

Why was the aristocracy so worried about poaching? They saw it as an attack on their own rights and as an invasion of their property. Since some poachers did not regard themselves as criminals, there was also a problem of class conflict, even of social rebellion: this might become very dangerous if not dealt with. Finally, there was the matter of tradition. The right to hunt had always belonged to the aristocracy. It was the most valued of all forms of recreation, practised by monarchs as well as nobles.

Punishments for poaching

Surprisingly, poaching was often treated less harshly before the mid eighteenth century than theft and robbery. This is possibly because there was no intrusion into a house (unlike burglary) or into a person's clothing (unlike picking pockets). Perhaps it was also because aristocrats often poached against each other. The punishment normally imposed was a fine or a term of imprisonment. An example of this can be seen in South East England.

Source 4

F.G. Emmison, *Elizabethan Life: Disorder*, details taken from Essex sessions and assize records.

A good deal of poaching took place in the parks of North Essex. Twice, in 1573 and 1576, Edward Earl of Oxford's 'Great Park' at Hedingham Castle was raided by two men of Yeldham and Toppesfield who shot at the wild and fallow deer, and by five men of Gestingthorpe who killed a doe. The five confessed and were ordered to remain in prison for three months and afterwards to be bound over to be of good behaviour for seven years.

If, however, the gamekeeper was wounded or killed by poachers, the poachers were usually hanged for murder. Nor would they have been eligible for benefit of clergy (see page 25).

Source 5

An original plan of Hedingham Castle and Park.

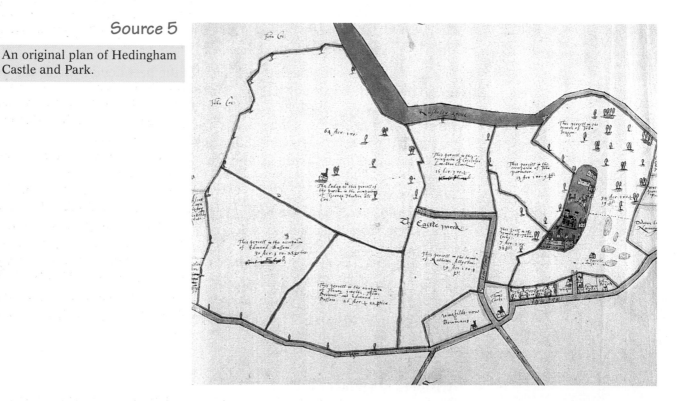

Questions

1. Divide the class into groups to prepare a detailed account of a raid on Hedingham Castle Park, and the outcome of the raid. Include the views of the poachers, gamekeeper, estate owner and the trial judge.

2. Debate the statement 'Hunting a deer was a worse crime than picking a pocket'.

3. Why was poaching considered to be a more serious crime in the period 1450–1750 than it would be today?

2.4 Smuggling

Why was smuggling a problem?

Smugglers illegally brought foreign goods into the country by not declaring them to the government officials on the coastline. The basic purpose of smuggling was to provide people with goods which were otherwise too expensive. Governments tried to protect British agriculture and industry by preventing foreign goods from being brought into the country, or making their prices very high. Smugglers released such goods on to the black market, where they were cheaper because the government taxes on goods had not been paid. Many parts of the English coastline were ideal for smuggling, from the coves of Cornwall and Devon to the river estuaries of Essex and Kent.

Source 1

Smugglers at work.

What was smuggled?

At the turn of the sixteenth century tobacco was the major item smuggled into England and Wales, mainly from French and Flemish ships lying off the coast of Cornwall. During the seventeenth century, however, tobacco became more plentiful since it was grown and exported by English colonies like Virginia in North America.

Attention then turned to tea, another commodity for which people had gained a taste. The Prime Minister, William Pitt, said in 1784 that duty had been paid on only 5.5 million pounds of the estimated 13 million pounds of tea consumed. Also brought in by small boats at night were quantities of wine, spirits, silk, and lace.

Attitudes to smuggling

To some people smugglers were seen as harmless adventurers with a taste for excitement and danger; to others they fulfilled a social function in keeping prices down. The attitude of this village parson is typical:

Source 2

An account by Parson Woodforde (29 March 1777).

> Andrews the smuggler brought me this night about 11 o'clock a bagg of Hyson Tea 6 pound weight. He frightened us a little by whistling under the parlour window just as we were going to bed. I gave him some Geneva and paid him for the tea at 10/6 [52$\frac{1}{2}$p] per pound.

Geneva A kind of gin.

The economist Adam Smith blamed the high government duties for smuggling (see Source 3). A smuggler was, therefore, no common criminal.

Source 3

Adam Smith, *Wealth of Nations*, volume II.

A person who, though no doubt highly blameable for violating the laws of his country, is frequently incapable of violating those of natural justice, and would have been, in every respect, an excellent citizen, had not the laws of his country made that a crime which nature never intended to be so.

On the other hand, government ministers argued that smugglers were inflicting serious damage on the country's economy. There is some truth in this. Taxation in this period was based on the payment of duties on goods, rather than on income. Smuggling therefore threatened to deprive the government of money that it needed to carry out its normal tasks, even to fight wars.

Also, most smugglers were concerned more about making a profit than about providing a social service. Much of the activity was organised by gangs, like the famous Hawkhursts. Some of these were willing, if necessary, to kill customs officials or to torture them to find out information. In some cases, individuals involved in smuggling were well set on a career of crime which involved other types of violence, like robbery. Dick Turpin was an example of this.

How was smuggling dealt with?

Punishment for smuggling

There was a range of punishments for smuggling, depending on the amount and value of the goods brought in, and the degree of violence committed. The death sentence was, however, often imposed as a deterrent to others. This was unpopular with the crowds, who supported any smugglers about to be executed. There would certainly have been some sympathy for James Holt:

Source 4

Extract from the *Northampton Mercury*, 20 July 1752.

James Holt, the Smuggler, behaved very penitently, but did not seem convinced that his Sentence was just, or that Smuggling merited Death. Amongst his last words were 'It is very hard to be hanged for Smuggling'.

penitent Feeling sorry for having committed a crime.

Did levels of smuggling go down?

Smuggling reached its peak during the eighteenth century. During the nineteenth century levels went down because successive governments reduced import duties and so lowered prices. Smuggling was therefore undercut by a policy of free trade.

On the other hand, smuggling changed its character in the twentieth century: gradually it came to mean the import of items which were illegal altogether, such as certain types of drugs and pornography.

Questions

1 Some historians have called smuggling a 'social crime', in that it broke the law but also helped people. Would you agree with this?

2 'Smuggling and poaching were crimes which were very close to each other'. Do you agree?

3 Were smugglers really any different from other criminals of the time?

Part 2: 1750–1900

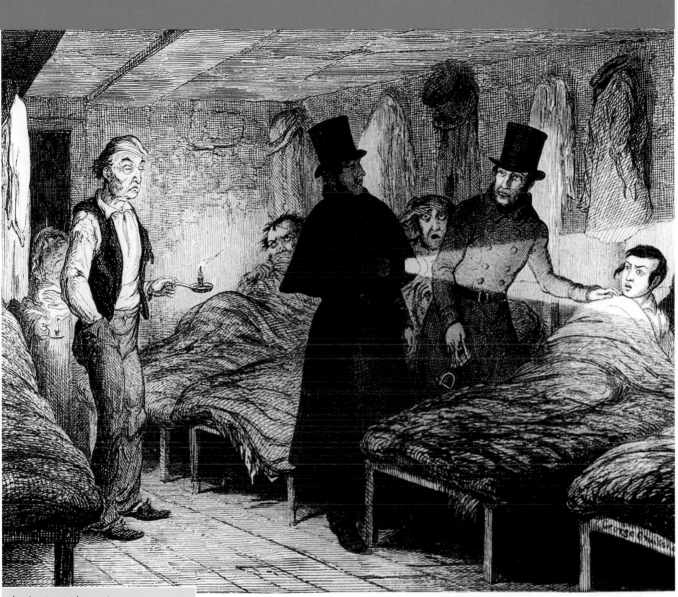

A nineteenth century illustration of a police raid on a 'threepenny lodging house', or court for poor people.

Part 2 deals with the period in which Britain became an industrial state, and in the process experienced a wide variety of problems. In this Part, crimes and punishment are treated separately and in more detail. The crimes are covered in Unit 3 (poaching, theft and violence) and Unit 4 (riots and conspiracy). Punishments are examined closely in Unit 5.

Unit 6 introduces a new part of the overall picture: the growth of a professional police force.

Unit 3 · Crimes against property and the person

3.1 Poaching

Comparisons with the period before 1750

We have already examined poaching as a crime between 1450 and 1750 (see pages 33–34). It should now be possible to work out both similarities and changes between the periods before and after 1750. After reading the rest of this section, try to work out examples of:

– an absence of any change (complete continuity)
– the same trend but speeded up (accelerated continuity)
– change in one respect but not in others (partial change)
– little or no continuity left (complete change).

During the nineteenth century poaching actually increased. Nationally it reached a peak in the 1830s and another in the 1870s. The counties which had the highest percentages of poaching compared with other offences were in East Anglia, especially Norfolk and Suffolk, and in the East Midlands, including Rutlandshire, Bedfordshire, Huntingdonshire and Nottinghamshire.

As before 1750, poachers of the late eighteenth and the nineteenth centuries had two main reasons for their activity: need and greed.

Source 1

A map showing the main areas of poaching in the nineteenth century.

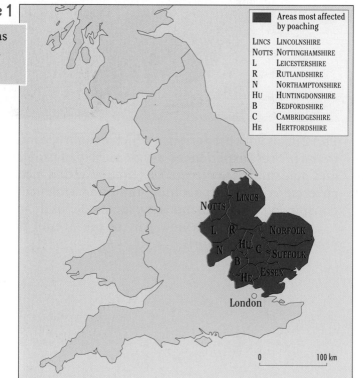

Areas most affected by poaching

LINCS	LINCOLNSHIRE
NOTTS	NOTTINGHAMSHIRE
L	LEICESTERSHIRE
R	RUTLANDSHIRE
N	NORTHAMPTONSHIRE
HU	HUNTINGDONSHIRE
B	BEDFORDSHIRE
C	CAMBRIDGESHIRE
HE	HERTFORDSHIRE

0   100 km

What were the reasons for poaching?

Poaching through need

Rural poverty continued to be widespread. More and more people were deprived of land as a result of the 'enclosure' movement of the eighteenth century. Similar enclosures had been made in Tudor times, when borders were put up to mark out private land. This greatly reduced the amount of common land available. Many people were forced to become labourers. Their wages were kept as low as possible, their diet got worse, and many reached the point of desperation, turning to poaching to survive.

For this reason, many people continued to see poaching as a 'social' crime and were sympathetic to those who committed it.

Source 2

D. Jones, *Crime, Protest, Community and Police in Nineteenth Century Britain*, (1982).

... Many sections of the community refused to treat the poacher as an ordinary criminal ... the working class regarded certain kinds of poachers as popular heroes. They rescued them from the hands of keepers and police and intimidated those people who took them to court.

A popular ballad from the early eighteenth century shows that some poachers saw themselves as martyrs:

Source 3

An extract from the ballad 'Keepers and Poachers'.

The judge and the jury unto him did say
'If you will confess, your sweet life shall be saved'.
'Oh no', then said William, 'that won't do at all,
For now you have got me I'll die for them all'.

Poaching through greed

Another point of view was that poaching was no different to theft and burglary: although tempting, poaching could never be justified. The police and estate owners mostly believed that there was no connection between poverty and poaching. They felt that, in any case, most of the profits were spent in pubs rather than on food. This was pointed out by a vicar in 1849.

Source 4

Rev. H. Worsley, *Juvenile Depravity*, (1849).

intemperance Excessive drinking.
retailer Supplier.

Intemperance and poaching act and re-act, the one vile habit on the other. 'Poaching', says a witness examined by the late Select Committee of the Game Laws, 'induces men and boys to be out at night, and brings them into connexion with individuals of very bad character, and carries them into those abominably bad places, the beer-shops ...' It is in the beer-shops that individuals of notorious character meet, it is here they concoct their plans ... the beer retailer is very frequently associated with the poachers, and to him they dispose of their plunder in payment for liquor.

A popular song stressed this moral lesson:

Source 5

From a ballad called 'A Shining Night, or Dick Daring, the Poacher'.

Be advised then ye young be advised too ye old,
To soberness honesty, industry hold,
For stealing and murder may rise it is clear
From a shining night if 'tis our delight in the season of the year.

Most of the poaching business that went on in pubs was organised by gangs, many of which were based in London. They grew steadily in size between 1830 and 1870, and representatives would make contacts with actual poachers in rural areas, like Norfolk, at places like the 'Chequers Inn' in Thetford. The temptations for poachers greatly increased during this period. Estate owners were deliberately building up fish and game stocks for the angling and shooting groups who were prepared to pay well for this popular pastime.

Dealing with poachers

Source 6

An early nineteenth century man trap.

At first the authorities tried to reduce poaching by a policy of deterrence. They introduced a variety of man-traps and spring-guns, the purpose of which was to kill, mutilate or break the legs of a poacher.

Punishments were also made worse. Poachers were sentenced to longer terms of imprisonment. The less fortunate were, from 1816, transported to places like New South Wales (Australia) for fourteen years. Between 1750 and 1820, more poachers than before were hanged, particularly those convicted of using a firearm or wounding a gamekeeper.

Further developments occurred during the nineteenth century. Some were definite improvements. During the 1830s, man-traps and spring-guns were made illegal, and an Act in 1883 allowed tenants to kill rabbits and hares on their own farms, so ending one of the most hated parts of the old game laws. On the other hand, the law remained heavily against the poacher. He could still be transported to a penal colony, or imprisoned for up to seven years. By the Poaching Prevention Act of 1862 anyone suspected of carrying poaching implements could be stopped and searched by the police. Poachers were able to argue that they were treated more harshly in the late nineteenth century than people accused of other forms of theft. This was in contrast to the period before 1750, and showed that the laws on poaching had changed more slowly than those applying to other forms of property.

Questions

1 This section provides comments on continuity and change in poaching before and after 1750. Give an example for each of:
   – complete continuity (an absence of any change)
   – accelerated continuity (the same trend but speeded up)
   – partial change (change in one respect but not in others)
   – complete change (little or no continuity left).

2 Were all the changes in the law on poaching after 1750 examples of 'progress'?

3 How useful are Sources 3 and 5 to the historian?

4 Was there a strong connection between poverty and poaching?

5 Class activity. Two groups are sitting in an inn in 1800. One group is discussing a poaching raid. Unknown to this group, another group is sitting on the other side of a thin wooden partition, overhearing every word. What does each group say?

3.2 Industrialisation and theft

Pages 27–32 dealt with theft and robbery between 1450 and 1750. As with poaching and other rural crimes, there was some continuity with the period 1750–1900. However, in the towns there was one particularly important change, which this section will deal with: the effect of industrialisation on crimes against property.

The reasons for theft

In general terms, the rate of theft increased steadily until the 1870s, when it levelled off and began to fall slightly. This trend was closely connected with the impact of the Industrial Revolution on towns and cities, especially London. Several factors were involved: squalor, poverty, drink, and the fear brought on by living in big cities.

Squalor

It is difficult to imagine the squalor in which the majority of the urban population lived during the nineteenth century. People lived in poorly ventilated cellars or dank and filthy buildings around courtyards, without basic services or sanitation.

 Source 1

An example of squalid housing in Glasgow. Many people lived in 'courts'. These were basic buildings built around small, often filthy yards.

Poverty

A late nineteenth century writer believed that most crime was committed by young men coming to London and finding themselves in desperate poverty. They went into a spiral of hopelessness.

Source 2

J.M. Rhodes, *Pauperism, Past and Present* 14 January 1891, a paper read to the Manchester Statistical Society.

s. Shorthand for shilling, an old coin equivalent to five pence.

They tried the decent courts for lodgings, and found that two rooms would cost 10s. per week. Food was dear and bad, water was bad, and in a short time their health suffered. Work was hard to get, and its wage was so low that they were soon in debt. They became more ill, and more despairing with the poisonous surroundings, the darkness and the long hours of work, and they were driven forth to seek a cheaper lodging. They found it in a court I knew well, a hotbed of crime and nameless horrors ... Then the demon drink seized them.

Some of these dens became well known as hotbeds of crime. As the police force became increasingly efficient, raids happened more and more often, and this meant the number of recorded crimes was likely to go up.

Poverty, which was widespread at the best of times, was disastrously affected by periods of economic recession. Societies become more vulnerable to these periods as they become industrialised. This is because they depend more on exporting goods abroad, and other countries sometimes have to reduce the quantity they take. Britain's economy was hit by recession between 1815 and 1819, from the mid 1820s to 1832, from the late 1830s to 1842, and in the late 1840s. These were precisely the periods when thefts of all kinds increased, especially in London. Those who were convicted in court usually offered poverty as a reason for their action.

Source 3

A statement made in court by William Dennison, aged 16 (from the *Old Bailey sessions papers*, 1816–17).

I do not wish to add falsehood to fraud. I own I took the coat, but it was from mere distress.

Some writers argued that the whole economic system was at fault, and drove people to commit crime. One of these was Frederick Engels, the son of a textile manufacturer, who worked in Manchester. In 1892 he published a book which said that the working class was exploited by the bourgeoisie (middle classes) within an economic structure known as 'capitalism'. In capitalist societies, industries tend to be owned privately by individuals or small groups, rather than by the state. So Engels argued that the working man could no more be blamed for committing crime than water could be for boiling.

Source 4

F. Engels, *The Conditions of the Working Class in England*, (1892).

volition Will, desire.
proletariat Working class.

Under the brutal and brutalising treatment of the bourgeoisie, the working-man becomes precisely as much a thing without volition as water, and is subject to the laws of Nature with precisely the same necessity; at a certain point all freedom ceases. Hence with the extension of the proletariat, crime has increased in England and the British nation has become the most criminal in the world.

Although Engels carefully watched and thought about people's working and living conditions, his views go well beyond those of historians and economists. Engels worked closely with Karl Marx, a man with strong revolutionary ideas, to develop a new economic and social way of thinking, known as communism.

Drink

A close connection has always been made between alcohol and crime. Many people found life in the slums of a city like London or Manchester so dreadful that they turned to drink to get away from reality. This became an addiction and provided an extra expense which could be met only through criminal earnings. So a 'vicious circle' was formed.

One of the strongest arguments linking drink and crime was provided in 1834:

Source 5

A gin palace (tavern or pub).

... In every shape and form, from theft, fraud and prostitution in the young, to burnings, robberies and more hardened offences in the old; by which the gaols and prisons, the hulks and convict transports are filled with inmates; and an enormous mass of human beings, who, under sober habits and moral training, would be sources of wealth and strength to the country, are transformed, chiefly through the remote or immediate influence of Intoxicating Drinks.

Source 6

Select Committee, appointed by the House of Commons, on Inquiry into Drunkenness, (1834).

hulk A ship acting as a prison for convicts.

What is left out of this document, however, is any reference to *why* so many people drank.

Fear

Cities filled people with fear much more than did the countryside. The poor and jobless feared unemployment, isolation and perhaps a lonely death. Involvement in crime provided many, especially the young, with a network of support, even a substitute for a family. According to a modern historian on crime in the nineteenth century:

Source 7

J.J. Tobias, *Crime and Industrial Society in the Nineteenth Century*.

The large towns during much of the Nineteenth century failed to provide the support which former country dwellers had known in the smaller communities from which they came. Entry into the criminal class was a means of finding support.

Fear also grew among the sections of the population who were likely to be the victims of crime. They feared what they saw as a huge underclass of 'degenerates', who were lazy and had no moral or religious values. They became ever more willing therefore to press charges, which was another reason for the steady increase in criminal statistics.

What types of theft?

Some forms of theft during the nineteenth century were traditional; others were new.

Picking pockets

One of the most common forms of theft was also one of the longest established. The subject of picking pockets has already been dealt with for the period up to 1750. But the ever-increasing size of London gave this type of criminal a new lease of life. Pickpockets worked wherever there were crowds, especially at public executions which might attract up to 200,000 people.

The best known account in literature of the activities of pickpockets is to be found in *Oliver Twist* by Charles Dickens. Dickens presents a story which is really based on the idea of the 'social crime', a crime that is due mainly to the social misfortune of the criminal. Oliver starts his life in a wretched workhouse before being sold as an apprentice to an undertaker, who treats him brutally. Fleeing to London, he meets the 'Artful Dodger' on the way.

Source 8

A description of the Artful Dodger from Dickens's *Oliver Twist*.

He was a snub-nosed, flat-browed, common-faced boy enough; and as dirty a juvenile as one would wish to see; but he had about him all the airs and manners of a man. He was short of his age: with rather bow-legs, and little, sharp, ugly eyes. His hat was stuck on the top of his head so lightly, that it threatened to fall off every moment ... He wore a man's coat, which reached nearly to his heels.

Oliver is taken by the Dodger to the leader of a pickpocket gang, Fagin. Within days, Oliver finds out the true purpose of Fagin's 'school'.

Source 9

A description of a theft, from Dickens's *Oliver Twist*.

What was Oliver's horror and alarm as he stood a few paces off, looking on with his eyelids as wide open as they would possibly go, to see the Dodger plunge his hand into the gentleman's pocket, and draw from thence a handkerchief; to see him hand the same to Charley Bates; and finally to behold them both running away around the corner at full speed!

Was Dickens, the author, going beyond the truth to impress his readers? Or is this an accurate description of a pickpocket? According to a modern historian:

Source 10

C. Emsley, *Crime and Society in England 1750–1900*, (1987).

Fagin's school for pickpockets appears to have had some basis in fact and it was confidently asserted that a child starting out as a ... street thief, if adept and well-trained, could rise to be a member of the exclusive group of professional pickpockets known as the 'swell mob'.

Their targets would be anything from purses to pocket handkerchiefs. Handkerchiefs were easiest, as they were worn hanging out of the pocket. A thief stealing between twenty and thirty of these in a week could live quite comfortably off the proceeds.

Stealing water

One form of theft was certainly new to the nineteenth century; stealing water was the direct result of urban squalor and inadequate water supplies. The problem was made even worse by the high charges placed by the water companies on the use of standpipes (water pipes in the street). This is illustrated by a letter to a newspaper in the middle of the nineteenth century.

Source 11

An extract from a letter to *The Morning Chronicle*, about 1850.

larceny Theft.

Where standpipes or public taps are erected, the charge by the water company is about 10s. a year for every house the inmates of which use the convenience. Of all the petty thefts which occur in Manchester, however, none ... are so common as larcenies from taps and pumps.

Company crimes

Far removed, by their wealth, from those people who had to steal water, were company 'fraudsters'. They too were a product of the Industrial Revolution. They made dishonest fortunes by falsely dealing with money invested in railway companies, mainly during the 'railway mania' of the 1840s. Sir Robert Peel tried to tidy up financial procedures in the 1844 Companies Act, which insisted on the auditing of accounts. But it was not until 100 years later that methods of protecting financial dealings were written down in any detail. Meanwhile, during the mid nineteenth century, it was likely that someone convicted of stealing water would receive a more severe sentence than a fraudster stealing people's life savings.

Questions

1 Write an account of the experiences of a young migrant to London in the 1840s. He or she starts out with high hopes, but quickly descends into a life of crime. Explain why.

2 How reliable is Source 4?

3 What is missing from Source 6? Add another paragraph to make it more complete.

4 Are Sources 8 and 9 primary or secondary? Give your reasons.

3.3 Crimes against the person

What types of crime?

A great deal has been written about crimes against the person in Victorian times. This section is confined to two themes. One is the change in attitudes to, and extent of, murder and assault. The other is the growth of a scandalous crime known as the 'white slave trade'.

Victorians and murder

Between the fifteenth and early nineteenth centuries murder had been considered an especially atrocious crime, but it had never caused the sort of morbid fascination which affected the Victorians. Murder trials became headline news, keenly followed by all levels of society. The two cartoons on pages 46 and 47 reflect the situation in the 1840s.

Various reasons can be given for this rise of interest in murder. Crime detection and policing had improved so much that more murders were solved. This meant that more were reported by the newspapers, which deliberately fed sensational accounts to the public. Hundreds of thousands of people also visited the 'chamber of horrors' at Madame Tussaud's waxworks in Baker Street. At the end of the century public interest was increased by the activities of Conan Doyle's fictional character, Sherlock Holmes, who was also based in Baker Street.

Another possible explanation is that murder was given a special status

Source 1

Punch magazine, 1849.

USEFUL SUNDAY LITERATURE FOR THE MASSES;
OR, MURDER MADE FAMILIAR.

Father of a Family (reads). "The wretched Murderer is supposed to have cut the throats of his three eldest Children, and then to have killed the Baby by beating it repeatedly with a Poker. * * * * * In person he is of a rather bloated appearance, with a bull neck, small eyes, broad large nose, and coarse vulgar mouth. His dress was a light blue coat, with brass buttons, elegant yellow summer vest, and pepper-and-salt trowsers. When at the Station House he expressed himself as being rather 'peckish,' and said he should like a Black Pudding, which, with a Cup of Coffee, was immediately procured for him."

once it became the only crime with a sentence of death (see page 60). An assize court, especially the Old Bailey, would appear particularly impressive and forbidding during a murder trial, especially when the judge put on a black cap to pronounce sentence of death.

The Victorians experienced waves of panic which were worse than those of earlier centuries. One of these occurred during the 1850s and 1860s, when there was a series of garottings, or stranglings. All of these received great publicity, and *Punch* magazine carried warnings in its cartoons about the dangers of living in certain areas. Another panic was caused by the 'Jack the Ripper' murders of the 1880s.

However, the reality was that the levels of homicide, including murder, gradually went down. Between 1857 and 1890 there were usually under

Source 2

Punch magazine, 1845.

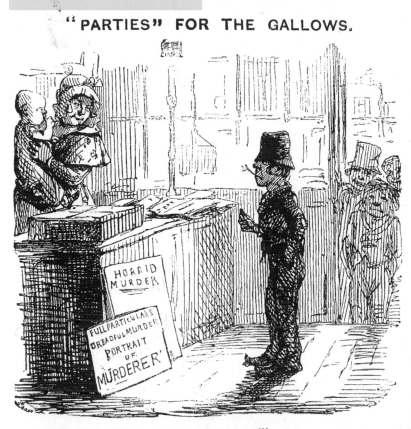

"PARTIES" FOR THE GALLOWS.

Newsvender.—" Now, my man, what is it?"
Boy.—" I vonts a nillustrated newspaper with a norrid murder and a lireness in it."

Source 3

From Walter Besant's book, *East London*, (1901).

consensus Agreement.

400 homicides reported to the police each year, and even fewer during the 1890s. Most victims knew their attackers, which meant that the actual danger of being assaulted and murdered in the streets was far smaller than Victorians feared. The same applied to Scotland and Ireland.

Assault in late Victorian England

The decrease in homicide figures was part of a more general trend towards fewer personal assaults.

To some extent, this shows the success of efforts made to deal with the social problems which were linked with many of the crimes of the period. Particularly important was the work of agencies formed to help specific parts of the population. Some were voluntary, like the Salvation Army, the Church Army, the Charity Organisation Society, the National Society for the Prevention of Cruelty to Children, Dr Barnardo's, and clubs for boys and girls. Government action included the development of education. All of these schemes helped to change people's attitudes and reduce the number of people vulnerable to criminal influences. According to Walter Besant:

There was a consensus that the influence of the schools had been to humanise the people in a manner actually visible to all. The results are before us. The children of today are in every respect better than they were twenty years ago.

The 'white slave trade'

Victorian England, as many historians have pointed out, was a society of 'double standards'. On the one hand, family life was strengthened and morality was considered more important than ever before. On the other hand, some Victorian men, including the 'respectable' and famous, secretly found sexual excitement in London's huge underworld. Prostitution had, of course, always existed; in fact it had been practised far more openly in the eighteenth century. However, the late Victorians were very concerned about the exploitation of young girls in what came to be called the 'white slave trade'.

A Select Committee provided evidence of this trade in 1882. It showed that girls had been lured by agents to Belgium, and placed in brothels there. The agents were paid about £12 for each girl provided. The girls were kept in debt to their new owners and were virtual prisoners. The report concluded with a depressing description of the situation in London itself (see Source 4).

Source 4

Report of the Select Committee of the House of Lords on the law relating to the protection of young girls, (1882).

The evidence before the Committee proves beyond doubt that juvenile prostitution, from an almost incredibly early age, is increasing to an appalling extent in England, and especially in London.

The report offered a number of reasons:

Various causes are assigned for this: a vicious demand for young girls; overcrowding in dwellings, and immorality arising therefrom; want of parental control ...; residence in some cases in brothels; the example and encouragement of other girls slightly older, and the sight of the dress and money, which their immoral habits have enabled them to obtain; the state of the streets in which little girls are allowed to run about...; and sometimes the contamination with vicious girls in schools.

A more strongly worded criticism of the exploitation of women was provided by a journalist of the time:

Source 5

W.T. Stead in the *Pall Mall Gazette*, (6 July 1885).

London's lust annually uses up many thousands of women, who are literally killed and made away with – living sacrifices slain in the service of vice.

He argued that this situation might be impossible to avoid, but that at least the young should be protected:

If daughters of the people must be served up as dainty morsels to minister to the passions of the rich, let them at least attain an age when they can understand the nature of the sacrifice which they are asked to make.

Questions

1 Examine Sources 1 and 2.
a How useful are cartoons as sources to the historian?
b Do Sources 1 and 2 trivialise a serious subject?
c Do Sources 1 and 2 make any assumptions about the sort of people interested in sensational murders?

2 Debate the statement 'Late Victorian England had become a safer place in which to live'.

3 Examine Source 3. What other reasons might have been included? Are these provided by Source 4?

Unit 4 · Crimes against authority

Britain was especially prone to disorder and riots between 1750 and 1850. This was partly because of the economic changes brought by the Agrarian and Industrial Revolutions, to which many people found it painful to adapt.

A riot occurred when a group of people took the law into their own hands and defied the authorities. There were many examples of this.

Four examples of riots, 1750–1900

1 The Gordon riots in 1780

Lord George Gordon objected to the 1778 Act which provided some relief for Britain's Catholic population, and enabled them to join the army. He argued that this was 'dangerous to the liberties of the people', and that the best way to be heard was to petition Parliament in 'a bold manner and show we mean to defend Protestantism with our lives'.

The march, which started from St George's Fields, south of the Thames, was at first peaceful. The marchers had blue cockades, anti-Catholic banners saying 'No Popery', and a huge rolled petition, which they carried on their shoulders. On their way they were joined by pickpockets, prostitutes, and some who were interested only in violence without knowing what the issue was. Many of the more peaceful marchers withdrew from the demonstration in disgust. The mob now got out of control and started to attack any members of Parliament who were suspected of being sympathetic to Catholics. According to a modern description:

Source 1

C. Hibbert, 'The Gordon riots' (in Purnell's *History of the English Speaking Peoples*).

> Lord Stormont was subjected to half an hour's kicking and pelting and his coach was utterly demolished. Lord Mansfield, the Lord Chief Justice, was assaulted in his carriage, all the windows of which were smashed ... The Bishop of Lincoln was seized by the throat with such ferocity that the blood gurgled from his mouth.

Part of the mob then burst into the House of Commons, while the rest chanted outside: 'Repeal!' and 'No Popery!'. Despite the noise, Parliament still debated Gordon's motion against the Catholics, and defeated him. Lord Gordon crept away humiliated.

The violence died down for the rest of the day but flared up again that night, as gangs of thugs roamed through London carrying hammers, pick-axes and other weapons. They burned property and Catholic churches, especially in Spitalfields and Moorfields. They then moved on to Downing Street, and set fire to the Lord Chief Justice's house in Bloomsbury Square. They also broke into distilleries and prisons.

The march to Parliament, and the outbreak of the Gordon riots.

The rioting lasted a week. During this time about 800 people were killed, 500 by the rioters and 300 by the troops trying to disperse them.

What were the riots all about? There was a mixture of different issues. The riots started as a march to get an Act repealed. This attracted violent people who had other complaints, against the authorities and against Irish immigrants who, they thought, were taking their jobs. It was unfortunate in this case that the Irish also happened to be Catholic. Above all, there were people in the mob who enjoyed the violence and welcomed the opportunity for rioting. The violence was made worse by the large quantities of cheap gin which were stolen.

2 The Luddite disturbances

These occurred during the first two decades of the nineteenth century. The Luddites' target was not so much people as machinery, which they felt was threatening the livelihood of the handworkers of the Midlands and the North. A modern historian writes that the riots:

Source 3

C.P. Hill, *British Economic and Social History 1700–1975*, (1977).

Reflected the natural hostility felt by uneducated men towards machines which were putting them out of work, as well as the unemployment caused by wartime fluctuations of trade.

fluctuation Rise and fall.

Three main areas of Britain were affected. In Lancashire, the Luddites burned down a weaving loom factory at West Houghton in 1812. Four men were hanged and seventeen were transported abroad. The Yorkshire sheep croppers smashed shearing frames with a hammer called 'Great Enoch'; for this, fourteen men were hanged. The Midland Luddites, operating in Derbyshire, Nottinghamshire and Leicestershire, smashed over 1000 frames. Seven men were transported.

Source 4

Luddite activities – 'The Nottingham Captain' plotting with agitators at the White Horse, Pentrich, Derbyshire.

The leadership of the riots remained something of a mystery. The Nottinghamshire Luddites distributed letters signed by 'King Ludd', 'Ned Ludd' or 'General Ludd', demanding better pay and the destruction of machinery. But, according to a modern historian, there was no such person:

Source 5

M. Thomis, *The Luddites*, 1970.

A single General Ludd there was none, though hopeful magistrates occasionally thought they had caught him.

The authorities took severe measures to deal with the disturbances. The destruction of machinery was made a hanging offence in 1812. 12,000 troops were called out to the affected counties in 1812, and there were twenty executions, one of a boy aged sixteen. Lord Byron, the poet, felt that these measures completely missed the point of the troubles.

Source 6

Byron's point of view in a House of Lords debate, from *Hansard*, the journal of Parliament, 27 February 1812.

penal code Criminal laws.

You call these men a mob ... Are we aware of our obligations to a mob? It is the mob that labour in your fields and serve in your houses, that man your navy, and recruit your army, that have enabled you to defy all the world, and can also defy you when neglect and calamity have driven them to despair ... Is there not blood enough upon your penal code, that more must be poured forth to ascend to Heaven and testify against you? ... Are these the remedies for a starving and desperate populace?

3 The Swing riots
These broke out in the Midlands and Southern England in 1830 as a result of hardship.

Source 7

G. Rudé, 'Captain Swing' in Purnell's *History of the English Speaking Peoples*.

It was a revolt against poverty and degradation, for higher wages, Poor Law allowances, and guaranteed employment; and in many counties it was also a protest against the introduction of farm machinery that threatened to throw men out of work.

After the Napoleonic Wars agricultural labourers faced increased rents, tithes (Church taxes) and government taxes. There was less work available for them, and the landowners kept their wages as low as possible. A special grievance was the use of threshing machines and other labour saving devices in the South, East Anglia and the Midlands.

The disturbances started when threshing machines were introduced in East Kent. Machinery was broken by labourers, who also sent threatening letters and demands for increases in wages. In Sussex, workhouses were attacked. Hay stacks were burned as the troubles spread westwards to Devon, Cornwall and the Welsh Borders. A second wave of problems started in Thatchenham in Berkshire. This was mainly a demand for higher wages, and it spread through the Home Counties. A third series of riots started in Norfolk, spreading southwards through East Anglia and then northwards to Yorkshire, ending at Carlisle.

The leader was said to be a man called Captain Swing. In reality he did not exist. The name was probably a reference to the 'swing flails' used for threshing crops at harvest time, before the introduction of machinery. The rioters sent out plenty of threatening letters to landlords, overseers and rent collectors, although hardly any direct violence was actually committed.

The government offered rewards for naming those people caught in the act of violence and the organisers of the riots. The courts were especially busy, sentencing 19 to death, 581 to deportation (the largest ever single batch) and 644 to imprisonment.

Source 8

A mob burning a farm in Kent during the Swing riots in 1830.

Source 9

A threatening letter sent by the Swing rioters.

> this is to inform you what you have to undergo Jentelmen if providing you Dont pull down your neshenes and rise the poor mens wages the maried men give tow and six pence a day a day the singel tow shilings or we will burn down your barns and you in them this is the last notis
>
> from W B

4 The Rebecca riots in 1839

A complicated series of disturbances broke out in South Wales in 1839. Most of the people involved were small-scale local farmers. They had already been badly affected by a combination of changes. These included the fall in the prices of farm produce, evictions by landowners, and increases in local taxes and tithes to the Church. The introduction of tollgates by turnpike trusts on roads was the last straw. Farmers fetching lime for their land found that they were charged toll money for each trip out and back.

These turnpikes were destroyed in a number of places. Some of the men involved dressed as women and their leader was known as Rebecca. A possible explanation was that the movement was influenced by the Old Testament of the Bible:

Source 10

An extract from *Genesis 24*, Old Testament.

And they blessed Rebekah, and said unto her, Thou art our sister, be thou the mother of thousands of millions, and let thy seed possess the gate of those which hate them.

THE WELSH RIOTERS.

Source 11

Two illustrations of the Rebecca riots.

By 1843 the whole of South Wales was affected. The rioters ordered the farmers not to pay tolls in the town of Carmarthen. There was one casualty: the person who ran a toll gate was killed when her house was burned down. The riots ended in 1844.

The authorities responded by sending some of those people involved to Australia. The government also set up an inquiry, which led to the following statement:

Source 12

The recommendation of a government report.

Farmers should not have to keep paying tolls for return journey. One payment should last for seven miles without another having to be paid.

This was not everything that the Rebecca rioters had wanted, but at least it was of some help to them.

1 'All four riots were carried out by people wanting reforms but having to extract them from unwilling authorities.' Is this true?

2 Write two letters to a newspaper about any one of the four riots in this section. The first letter should defend the rioters. Decide for yourself what viewpoint the second letter should take.

3 In three of the four riots there was a lack of strong leadership. Did this matter?

4 List the four riots in the order in which you think they frightened the authorities, from most to least. Give reasons for your choice.

5 Compare the ways in which the authorities reacted to the four riots.

6 Which of the four riots do you find most interesting? What questions would you ask in order to learn more about it?

4.2 Conspiracy

Between 1790 and the late 1840s the British government was worried about the possibility of being overthrown by a revolution. After all, this happened three times in France during this period, and many other countries in Europe were affected in the same way.

The government was therefore always on the look-out for signs of 'conspiracy', or the formation of organisations which seemed likely to go against authority. It was, however, so concerned about its security that it did not properly distinguish between different types of organisation or activity. Some organisations were set up as responses to economic hardship, or as peaceful demands for the vote. Others were set up as more deliberate attempts to cause a disturbance or a crisis.

On the whole, the government played safe by applying tough, general laws to them all. This happened especially during the ministries of William Pitt and Lord Liverpool.

Source 1

Anti-conspiracy measures of William Pitt.

seditious Having no respect for authority.
trade union Organisation of workers to protect their interests.

Year	Name of Bill or Act	What it meant
1795	Treasonable Practices Bill	Defined treason in a very general way.
1795	Seditious Meetings Bill	Placed restrictions on public assembly for any purpose.
1799	Corresponding Act	Banned any political correspondence (communication) with revolutionary France.
1799, 1800	Combination Acts	Prohibited (banned) any trade union ('combination') of workmen.

Source 2

William Pitt.

Source 3

Lord Liverpool.

Source 4

Anti-conspiracy measures of Lord Liverpool.

habeas corpus The right not to be held in prison without a trial.

Year	Name of Bill or Act	What it meant
1817	Suspension of 'habeas corpus'	Prisoners could be detained without trial.
1819	Six Acts	Empowered magistrates to search houses for firearms and seditious literature; prohibited military drilling by civilians; imposed restrictions on political meetings; enabled trials to take place without juries; increased taxes on pamphlets and newspapers.

It is true that Liverpool's government did repeal the Combination Acts, so allowing trade unions to be formed, but as we shall see, it was still possible for him to clamp down on trade union activity.

Two examples of conspiracy

The rest of this section looks at two specific examples of 'conspiracy'. The first example was a genuine threat to the government. The second was a terrible miscarriage of justice.

1 The Cato Street conspiracy, February 1820

This was led by Arthur Thistlewood, who planned to blow up the Prime Minister and his cabinet (government) while they were dining in Lord Harrowby's house. The government discovered the plot through a spy, and the conspirators were arrested in Cato Street (near Edgware Road in London). Thistlewood and the other conspirators resisted arrest, killed a policeman and escaped.

Mrs Arbuthnot gave the following account of the plans, based on an evening conversation with the Duke of Wellington:

Source 5

The Journal of Mrs Arbuthnot, (1820). Mrs Arbuthnot was the wife of a Tory M.P. She was interested in politics and kept a detailed record.

> He [the Duke of Wellington] said their plan had been, after completing the murder of the Ministers, to attack Coutts' and Childs' banking houses to get money, to set fire to several houses, to collect a mob, to break open the gun-smith's shop to arm them, to seize six pieces of artillery which they knew were in the artillery ground, and for which they had provided ammunition, to seize on the Bank and Mansion House and to murder everybody that attempted to leave London.

Thistlewood himself was beheaded, three others hanged, and six were transported to Botany Bay in New South Wales (Australia).

2 The Tolpuddle Martyrs

Trade unions were accepted again from 1824, when the Combination Acts were repealed by Lord Liverpool's government. However, another law, passed in 1825, put some restrictions on trade unionists, preventing them from exerting too much influence on the people they worked with. Still, trade unions were now legal and began to spring up. The largest was the Grand National Consolidated Trades Union (GNCTU) in 1833.

Employers continued to regard trade unions with a deep lack of trust, and took whatever measures against them that the law offered. Their best chance of defeating workers was to accuse trade unions of 'conspiracy'. This happened in the 1830s in Dorset. In 1833 a group of 40 agricultural workers in Tolpuddle set up a branch of the Friendly Society of Agricultural Labourers. The organiser was James Loveless, a 28-year-old labourer, who hoped that the branch would eventually join with the larger GNCTU. The employers in Tolpuddle feared that the large union would press them for better conditions and higher wages, and so they looked for a way of taking legal action against it.

Local farming employers discovered that the new union was using a secret initiation ceremony and an oath of allegiance, described in Source 6 by a modern historian.

Source 6

P. Gregg, *A Social and Economic History of Britain 1760–1972*, (7th edition, 1973).

> A ritual and initiation ceremony were adopted. The village painter made a life-size figure of a skeleton. James Loveless clothed himself in a white surplice, intending members were blindfolded, took an oath of secrecy, and pledged themselves to carry out the aims of the union.

The employers argued that such oaths were against an Act of 1797. The Home Office and local magistrates agreed to support their action, and in 1834 those workers who had taken the oaths were tried at Dorchester and sentenced to seven years' transportation. It was now possible for other employers to put people off joining unions, by using an Act which had really been designed to deal with military threats like the Nore Mutiny, when complaints were made about conditions in the Royal Navy.

What was the effect of this? On the one hand it proved to be a deterrent against further 'combination'. Numbers of unions declined and the GNCTU ended. On the other hand, there was a national outrage against the injustice suffered by the Tolpuddle labourers. They became the subject of a campaign of public meetings and a petition carrying 250,000 signatures. Meetings were held with numbers estimated by The Times at 30,000 and by trade unionists at between 100,000 and 200,000. Eventually, in 1836, the government agreed to allow the Tolpuddle labourers to return from the harsh lives they had been forced to live in Botany Bay and Tasmania, Australia.

Questions

1 How useful and reliable would the historian find Source 5?

2 What similarities and differences can you suggest between Arthur Thistlewood and Guy Fawkes?

3 What does the Tolpuddle Martyr episode show us about the attitudes and policy of the authorities?

4 Why are the Tolpuddle labourers referred to as 'Martyrs'? Did they have anything in common with the religious martyrs of the reigns of Mary I and Elizabeth I? (See also pages 10–12.)

Unit 5 · Punishment

How extensive was capital punishment?

Hanging offences in the eighteenth century

In the eighteenth century a person could be hanged for over 200 offences, including murder, rape, robbery, conspiracy, riotous behaviour, theft of a horse or sheep, most forms of burglary, and picking pockets. Two of the more unusual capital offences were damaging Westminster Bridge and impersonating a Chelsea Pensioner.

How many people were hanged?

It is a startling thought that 90 per cent of all criminals hanged were under 21 and that some were as young as 10. First-time offenders were sometimes let off. The rest had probably started as pickpockets and had regularly broken the law. These were shown no mercy.

We do not know the total number of people hanged in Britain in the period starting from 1750, but statistics have been drawn up for a number of counties in England. A typical example is Surrey.

Source 1

The number of people executed in Surrey between 1749 and 1802.

Crime	Number of executions					
	1749–75		1776–87		1788–1802	
	M	F	M	F	M	F
Robbery	65	0	37	4	21	0
Burglary	20	0	27	0	20	1
Horse theft	7	0	5	0	8	0
Sheep theft	1	0	0	0	4	2
Housebreaking	1	0	3	0	3	0
Picking pockets	1	0	0	0	0	0
Other theft	0	0	5	1	9	2
Murder	17	1	5	1	2	0
Rape	1	0	0	0	1	0
Coining/forgery	5	0	3	0	5	1
Riot	0	0	0	0	2	0
Returning from transportation	3	0	0	0	1	0

M = Male F = Female

This table shows that the crimes most frequently punished by death were robbery and burglary. This was especially the case when they were carried out by gangs.

How executions were carried out

Almost all towns had a place of public execution with a scaffold as a permanent feature. In London, condemned criminals were taken in the back of a cart from the courts in the area called the City to Tyburn (now Speaker's Corner at Marble Arch).

On the way, they were insulted or pelted by crowds. At Tyburn there was a large gallows known as the 'Three-Legged Mare' on which many criminals could be hanged at the same time. A Bow Street Runner (an early type of policeman) said that, between 1781 and 1786 there was not:

Source 2

A Bow Street Runner's observations.

An execution wherein we did not grace that unfortunate gibbet with ten, twelve, to thirteen, sixteen and twenty; and forty I saw at twice.

The condemned criminal would be accompanied to the gallows by a clergyman, who tried to persuade him to make a full public apology and confession. Death would then be by strangulation and the criminal's relatives would often pull on his or her feet to speed up the death.

From 1783 most executions in London were transferred to a site just outside Newgate prison (see Source 3). At the same time, a more humane method of hanging was introduced to replace strangulation. The sudden removal of the platform resulted in the neck being broken so that death was almost immediate.

Source 3

An execution at Newgate.

What did people think of capital punishment?

Very few people between 1750 and 1900 argued that hanging should not be used as a punishment. But two questions were often discussed:
Were too many offences punishable by hanging?
Should hanging be carried out in public?

Cases for and against hanging offences

Those people who believed that hanging should be used for all except the most minor offences were arguing on the basis of deterrence. They said that if hanging was reduced, crime would go up. If anything, the punishment should be made more severe. A Surrey Justice of the Peace, Martin Madan, said that this would actually save lives in the long run.

Those people who felt that the number of capital offences should be reduced had two arguments. Firstly, deterrence only worked if there was a likelihood of being caught; so what really needed to be increased was not the number of executions but the number of law-enforcement officials. Secondly, many criminals were acquitted even if they had committed minor offences, because the juries did not want them to hang. Where was the justice here?

The case for reducing the number of capital offences proved the more convincing. In the 1820s the Tory Home Secretary, Sir Robert Peel, abolished the death penalty for 180 types of offence. He also allowed the judge to decide whether or not to apply the death sentence for most of the remaining ones. By 1837 hanging was used mainly for murder or treason, and only for these offences from the 1860s.

Cases for and against public execution

In the eighteenth century most judges and M.P.s were in favour of executions being carried out in public. Some went further and argued that hanging was not enough of a deterrent, since many condemned criminals went to the gallows showing that they were bold and could not care less. One writer believed that death should be made more painful.

Source 4

George Olyffe, *An Essay Humbly Offer'd, for an Act of Parliament to prevent Capital Crimes, and the Loss of Many Lives, and to Promote a desirable Improvement and Blessing in the Nation*, (1731).

imbibe Take in.

... By seeing the Tortures of the Delinquents, they may be terrified into Obedience of the Law; for those criminals are not sufficiently deterr'd from the Dread of Hanging, as they have imbib'd the notion that it is an easy Death.

There was even a suggestion that execution should be by the bite of a rabid dog.

Voices were also raised *against* public executions. One of these was a reporter on criminal cases.

Source 5

From an article in *Gentleman's Magazine*, (1786).

Nothing could be more affecting than to hear judgement of death pronounced against a little army of fellow creatures, to be hanged like dogs.

Even later, when hanging was used mainly as a punishment for murder, there were people against carrying it out in public. In November 1849, the novelist Charles Dickens was sickened by what he saw outside Newgate prison before and after the execution of George and Maria Manning.

Source 6

Charles Dickens's letter to *The Times*, 14 November 1849.

I went there with the intention of observing the crowd gathered to behold it ... I believe that a sight so inconceivably awful as the wickedness and levity of the immense crowd collected at the execution this morning could be imagined by no man ... The horrors of the gibbet and of the crime which brought the wretched murderers to it, faded in my mind before the atrocious bearing, looks and language, of the assembled spectators … I am solemnly convinced that nothing that ingenuity could devise to be done in this city … could work such ruin as one public execution, and I stand astounded and appalled by the wickedness it exhibits.

Dickens watched the crowd 'all through the night, and continuously from daybreak until after the spectacle was over'. He was affected by the appalling behaviour of the children, by the 'thieves, low prostitutes, ruffians, and vagabonds of every kind'. There were 'fightings', 'brutal jokes' and 'tumultuous demonstrations of indecent delight'.

How were the authorities affected by arguments like this? During the eighteenth century they were convinced that public executions should remain, but that the disgrace behind them should be increased. This would be done not by making death more painful, but by refusing the relatives permission to provide a proper burial. Instead, some corpses were handed over to surgeons for dissection.

The 1752 Murder Act instructed judges to include dissection as part of the sentence for murderers. This was:

Source 7

Murder Act, 1752.

heinous Wicked.
perpetrate Perform, carry out.
the metropolis London.

To impress a just horror in the mind of the offender, and on the minds of all such as shall be present, of the heinous crime of murder, which has of late been more frequently perpetrated than formerly, particularly in and near the metropolis.

THE FOUR STAGES OF CRUELTY.

THE REWARD OF CRUELTY.

Source 8

Dissecting a criminal's corpse, an engraving from Hogarth's *The Reward of Cruelty*, 1751.

Another, much older, method of disgrace was to display the body in chains for some weeks near the spot of the crime or the criminal's place of residence. This was brought back after 1748 as an additional deterrent against murder. A Swiss visitor wrote that:

Source 9

The letters of Monsieur César de Saussure to his family.

> The lower classes do not consider it a great disgrace to be simply hanged, but have a great horror of hanging in chains, and the shame of it is terrible for the relatives of the condemned.

By the middle of the nineteenth century, however, the view of most authorities was beginning to move the other way. Writers like Dickens opened their eyes to the dangerous effects of such sights on the people who gathered to watch them. Public executions at Newgate attracted crowds of 200,000 or more. These were crushed into the narrow streets around St Paul's Cathedral, and this provided a perfect opportunity for pickpockets and prostitutes, even for armed robbers. Usually barricades were set up between the crowds and the scaffold to prevent any interference with the course of justice. But this also prevented the police from helping those under attack in the crowd.

It had therefore become clear that crime actually increased whenever there was a public hanging. At last, the government of Benjamin Disraeli decided in 1868 that executions should be removed from the public's gaze and carried out behind prison walls.

Source 10

An execution in St Albans behind prison walls, 1899.

Questions

1   Which of the following reasons was strongest for the use of capital punishment before 1900: retribution, deterrence or removal? Explain your answer.

2   'Ending public executions meant that the authorities did not think it worked as a deterrent'. Do you agree with this?

3   Were attitudes to capital punishment in the eighteenth century evidence that England was an uncivilised country?

4   Write a dialogue (or act out a scene) between members of a jury having to decide on the innocence or guilt of a woman accused of picking pockets in 1760. What is your verdict? Do the same for the same offence in 1860.

5.2 Imprisonment

The purpose and nature of imprisonment

The idea of houses of correction had started during the Tudor period to deal with vagrants and the able-bodied poor. As a punishment, however, imprisonment was less widely used than whipping, or branding, or even hanging. Then, in 1706, an Act of Parliament enabled judges to send criminals who had successfully claimed benefit of the clergy to a house of correction for up to two years. This was a major step forward.

Advantages of imprisonment
Two major advantages of imprisonment became more and more clear in the eighteenth century.

1 Previously, there had been no real alternative to sentencing offenders to death, or releasing them back into society. This meant that people committing smaller crimes often got off without any punishment, because the authorities might think it was unfair to send them to the gallows. Juries, too, were likely to acquit people, for the same reason. With imprisonment as an alternative, it was no longer necessary to do this.

2 Imprisonment could be used to make the rehabilitation of the offender part of the punishment.

Source 1

Thomas Robe, *Some Considerations for rendering the Punishment of Criminals more effectual*, (1733).

Thus Justice managed as an Act of Mercy, by slow, and yet effectual Methods, will bring Criminals to a sense of their Crimes, and beget in them such a Habit of Industry, as in the end will make them useful, if not honest, Members of the Publick.

By the end of the eighteenth century, imprisonment had become the punishment most commonly used for convicted criminals (60% of those in Surrey and 43% in Sussex). This seemed to show a more humane attitude.

Unfortunately there were still major problems, the worst one being prison conditions.

Life in prisons
In the eighteenth and early nineteenth centuries, most prisons were horrible places. They were never cleaned out, so they were infested with lice and other parasites, and were ideal for the spread of deadly diseases like typhus (often called 'gaol fever'). A vivid description was provided in 1777 of prisoners at Newgate:

Source 2

John Howard, a Bedfordshire magistrate, *The State of the Prisons in England and Wales*'.

countenance Face.
emaciated Thin.

The sallow meagre countenances declare, without words, that they are very miserable; many who went in healthy, are in a few months changed to emaciated dejected objects. Some are seen pining under diseases ... expiring on the floors, in loathsome cells, of pestilential fevers, and the confluent smallpox.

He also showed that prisoners were only given 102 ounces of bread per week. Many prisons had no water, and prisoners might be limited to three pints per day. Many cells were entirely or partially underground, damp or waterlogged. There were no sewers, and sanitation was not properly attended to. Ventilation was bad because many cell windows were blocked up by prison guards to avoid payment of 'window tax'. There was little or no straw, and this was rarely changed.

Conditions were just as bad for women at Newgate. Thomas Buxton's Inquiry (1818) described how over 300, some untried, some under sentence of death, crowded into two wards and two cells:

Source 3

Buxton, *An Inquiry whether Crime and Misery are produced or prevented by our present System of Prison Discipline*, (1818).

> They all slept on the floor; at times one hundred and twenty in a ward, without so much as a mat for bedding; and many of them were very nearly naked ... Everything was filthy to excess, and the smell was quite disgusting.

Buxton also noticed 'the ferocious manners and expressions of the women towards each other'.

Even more unpleasant were the hulks, which took in the overflow of people from the prisons. First used in 1776, these were disused warships, each crammed with up to 400 chained convicts. They were moored by naval arsenals or dockyards, at places like Portsmouth, Sheerness, Chatham, Woolwich and Deptford.

Source 4

Illustration of a hulk.

Changes in prison conditions

The demand for prison improvements

A number of individuals kept up the pressure on the government to reform these conditions.

The first was Jonas Hanway, who believed that prisoners would be most likely to be rehabilitated by a combination of improved hygiene and Christian ideas. His main proposals were to arrange for separate accommodation for each prisoner and daily visits from a chaplain.

He was followed by John Howard, who published a report called *State of the Prisons in England and Wales* (see Source 2). He thought that the cause of the appalling conditions was not 'cruelty' so much as neglect and 'inattention' by the authorities. What was needed was proper work and decent food. Howard also recommended that prison guards should receive regular payment from the authorities, instead of fees from prisoners. Regulations should be introduced to improve sanitary conditions and to control the behaviour of prisoners. Above all, prisons should receive regular visits from chaplains, surgeons and inspectors. Unfortunately, little was done about this at the time. Howard died in 1790, and the French Revolution and Wars diverted attention away from reform.

The campaign was picked up again after the return of peace in 1815. Elizabeth Fry, a Quaker minister and preacher, set up an organisation to try to improve conditions for women inmates in Newgate prison. According to a Report in 1818, Elizabeth Fry's visits to Newgate and her personal influence brought about a transformation.

Source 5

Buxton's *Inquiry*.

licentiousness Having no sexual morals.
sobriety Soberness.
apparel Clothing.

Riot, licentiousness, and filth, exchanged for order, sobriety, and comparative neatness in the chamber, the apparel, and the persons of the prisoners. They saw no more an assemblage of abandoned and shameless creatures, half-naked and half-drunk ... this hell upon earth already exhibited the appearance of an industrious manufactory, or a well regulated family.

Nineteenth century reforms

Governments after 1815 showed more willingness to accept some of the arguments of the reformers. Particularly important were the measures of Peel. The Gaols Act of 1823 started the payment of salaries to gaolers (prison officers), the grading of prisoners for work, regular inspection of prisons and visits from chaplains and surgeons. Female prisoners were to be under the authority of women warders. Basic education was also to be provided. More reforms followed in due course. During the 1830s prisoners were allowed separate cells and more work was provided, while in 1835 inspectors of prisons were appointed. Unfortunately, these changes applied only to prisons in the larger towns. Smaller gaols and debtors' prisons were not reformed in the same way.

Meanwhile, the size of the prison population was steadily increasing. This was due partly to improved detection, and partly to the fall in the number of other forms of punishment.

The government was therefore forced to take another, and more sweeping set of measures. The most important of these was the largest prison-building programme in the whole of English history, inspired by the ideas of Joshua Jebb, the Surveyor General of Prisons. He believed that there should be one prisoner per cell. His design also allowed for cells to be organised into 'wings', which spread outwards from a central hub (see Source 6): this meant easier supervision by guards.

The first prison of this type was Pentonville in London, opened in 1842 to accommodate 500 inmates. Others followed, including Portland in 1849, Dartmoor (1850), Portsmouth (1852), Brixton (1853) and Chatham (1856). Between 1842 and 1850, 50 prisons were built or rebuilt; by 1877 the figure had reached 90.

Source 6

Pentonville prison, London. The first prison built in the new style.

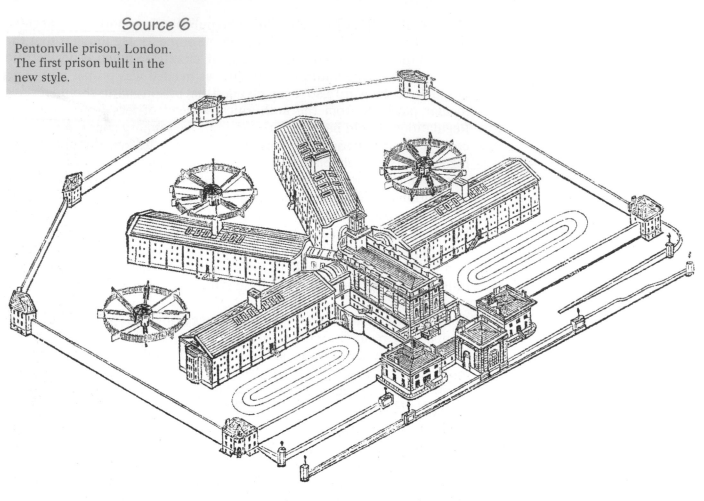

Some prisons, however, continued to use tough forms of punishment, like treadmills, for prisoners who did not obey the rules. A modern historian describes what happened at Wormwood Scrubs prison, in London.

Source 7

K. Chesney, *The Victorian Underworld*, (1970).

Here the treadmills were close compartments in which a prisoner remained for a quarter of an hour at a time, vigorously treading down a wheel of twenty-four steps at a fixed rate. They were arranged in rows..., the wheels turning a long axle attached to an ingenious apparatus of air-vanes that allowed it to revolve at exactly the right, agonising speed. The men were unable to get a firm grip which made the process very tiring.

The speed of the treadmill was controlled by turning a 'screw'. This soon became a nickname for all prison officers. A second form of punishment was 'shot drill', which meant carrying heavy cannon balls from one part of the prison yard to another. A third form was the 'crank' which meant turning a handle attached to a heavy drum filled with sand. Finally, of course, there were the traditional forms of flogging and birching.

Treatment of young offenders

In the early nineteenth century children were imprisoned for some offences along with adults. Some prisons attempted to introduce a separate way of treating children, such as Warwick Gaol in 1819. Some institutions were set up especially for children by the Prison Discipline Society, but these did not have enough money to run properly. Children were also to be found on

Source 8

A treadmill at Wormwood
Scrubs prison, around 1890.

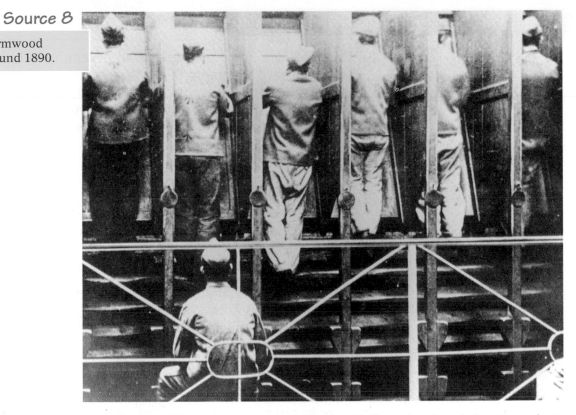

the hulks (ship prisons), especially the 'Bellerephon' and the 'Euryalus',
where there was brutality and bullying by older boys.

Parkhurst prison, on the Isle of Wight, was the first serious attempt in
1838 to provide a separate establishment for boys. At first the treatment of
the boys was very strict, and included leg irons and restricted diet.
Gradually, however, conditions improved and agricultural and industrial
work was introduced.

Questions

1 Write a description of life in Newgate prison in 1820:
a from the point of view of the prisoners
b from the point of view of the prison warders.

2 How important was each of the following as a reason for government
reforms of prisons in the nineteenth century?
a the more humane treatment of prisoners
b the more effective control over prisoners
c the better management of prisons
d the criticisms of John Howard
e the actions taken by Elizabeth Fry
f the rise in the prison population.
Give reasons for your choice.

3 Why did prison reformers act as they did?

5.3 Transportation

Criminals who were 'transported' were sent, usually for life, to a penal colony in the far corners of the British Empire. Transportation started during the seventeenth century and reached its peak in the late eighteenth and early nineteenth centuries. It went through two quite separate stages, the first involving North America and the second Australia.

Where and when?

Transportation to North America

From 1654 onwards, some criminals who received a reprieve from their death sentence were sent to work on the plantations in North America and the West Indies. Then an Act of Parliament in 1718 stated that transportation should be more widely used, as an alternative to existing punishments. The opening section of this Act stated that:

Source 1

An Act of Parliament in 1718.

The punishments inflicted by the laws now in force against the offences of robbery, larceny and other felonious taking and stealing of money and goods, have not proved effectual to deter wicked and evil-disposed persons from being guilty of the said crimes.

Transportation reached its peak during the 1750s and 1760s but came to a sudden end in the 1770s. The main reason for this was the revolt of the thirteen colonies against British rule. The newly independent United States naturally refused to take in any more of Britain's convict population. For a while this caused a serious problem to the British authorities because prisons were overflowing. A short-term solution was to use hulks, but in the longer term they had to find somewhere else to replace North America.

Transportation to Australia

The idea of transportation to Australia is thought to have started with Joseph Banks, botanist on one of Captain Cook's expeditions. He believed in 1779 that Botany Bay would make a suitable settlement. William Pitt

Source 2

A convict settlement on Norfolk Island.

and the Home Secretary, Lord Sydney, took action and the first convicts were landed in 1788. Other settlements followed, including Norfolk Island and Port Jackson.

Transportation was now used as a punishment for a wide range of offences, including thefts of under a shilling, or stealing a shroud out of a grave or fish from a pond. Alternatively, people could be transported for various forms of social protest; examples of this are the Luddites and the Tolpuddle Martyrs.

For and against transportation

Arguments in favour of transportation

The most important advantage of transportation was that it was an alternative to both hanging and imprisonment. It meant that judges did not have to inflict the death sentence for small burglaries. At the same time, they could be sure of removing the criminal from English society and of setting an example to others.

It also provided a way of reducing some of the pressures on England's prisons. Between 1805 and 1842 the population doubled and crime increased to five times the previous level. Before the era of prison-building from the 1840s onwards, there was simply no space for the extra numbers of people sentenced for non-capital offences.

On the other hand, there was always a need for more people in the more remote parts of the British Empire: men and women who were tough and energetic might do well in the wilderness. They might even improve themselves. Many convicts in Australia were eventually given their freedom and became small landowners. According to some descriptions, life was not too bad.

Source 3

A letter from Henry Tingley to his father, 1835.

We have as much to eat as we like, as some masters are a great deal better than others. All a man has got to mind is to keep a still tongue in his head, and do his master's duty, and then he is looked upon as if he were at home; but if he don't, he may as well be hung at once, for they would take you to the magistrates court and get 100 of lashes, and then get sent to a place called Port Arthur to work in irons for two or three years ... then, thank God for it, I am doing a great deal better than ever I was at home, only for the wanting you with me, that is all my uncomfortableness is in being away from you.

Arguments against transportation

There were, however, plenty of voices raised against transportation in the nineteenth century. Some local authorities complained that the families of those transported would be left destitute (penniless); they would therefore have to be supported from the rates provided by local tax payers. Others were convinced that transported criminals were returning illegally to England. As they faced immediate hanging if discovered, they had nothing to lose by following a life of crime. This often meant the organisation of dangerous gangs.

There were also strong humanitarian arguments against transportation. These were presented by a series of Select Committees of the House of Commons in 1810–12, 1819, 1837–8, 1847, 1856, 1861 and by Royal Commission, appointed by the government in 1863.

Source 4

Extract from the report of the 1837 Select Committee.

Your Committee consider ... that Transportation is not a simple punishment, but rather a series of punishments, embracing every degree of human suffering, from the lowest, consisting of a slight restraint upon freedom of action, to the highest, consisting of long and tedious torture; and that the average amount of pain inflicted upon offenders in consequence of a sentence of Transportation is very considerable.

The same committee argued that it was not even a good deterrent, since people in England knew very little about the life led by convicts in Australia.

Source 5

Select Committee of 1837.

testimony Evidence.
felon Criminal.

It is proved beyond a doubt, by the testimony of every witness best acquainted with the actual condition of convicts, and likewise by numerous facts stated in the evidence ... that most persons in this country, whether belonging to the criminal population, or connected with the administration of justice, are ignorant of the real amount of suffering inflicted upon a transported felon, and underrate the severity of the punishment of Transportation ... those convicts who write to their friends an account of their own fate, are generally persons who have been fortunate in the lottery of punishment, and truly describe their lot in flattering terms.

Transportation also led to degrading conditions on board ships. Men were chained up in steel cages for months on end before reaching their destination, as is shown in Sources 6 and 7.

Source 6

The interior of a convict ship.

Source 7

Leg-irons used in a convict ship.

Finally, the colonies themselves were strongly against being used as a 'dumping ground' for England's unwanted criminals. The North American colonists were already beginning to protest by 1700 and the population of New South Wales in Australia by 1820. Escaped convicts undoubtedly increased the level of crime in Australia. The most famous examples were the bushrangers, the Australian equivalent of the highwaymen in England. One of these was 'Bold Jack Donahoe' who was eventually killed in a shoot-out with the authorities.

The end of transportation

The British government soon came under heavy pressure from the Select Committees and from the authorities in New South Wales, Queensland and Tasmania. It therefore decided to stop transportation to Australia from 1840 onwards.

Questions

1. Why were there two stages in the growth of transportation? In what ways were these two stages similar and in what ways were they different?

2. Sir John Fielding, the eighteenth century Justice of the Peace, said that transportation was 'the wisest punishment we have'. Was he right?

3. Read Sources 3 and 5 on the life led by convicts in Australia. What are the similarities and differences? How reliable is Source 3 as an account of the lives of all convicts? Give several reasons.

4. Using the information and sources in this section write, or act out, a debate which might have taken place in the House of Commons in the 1830s about whether or not to continue transporting convicts to Australia.

5.4 Other punishments

Fines

One of the main forms of punishment today is the fine. This was also used in the eighteenth century, but on a much smaller scale and in a different way.

For the poor, fines might be used for smaller game offences, petty fraud, or defamation of (insulting) officials or the monarch. One of the problems, however, was the small amount earned by labourers. Another was the high rate of unemployment; it was, for example, quite unrealistic to expect a vagrant to pay a fine. This meant that a petty criminal who could not pay up would probably be imprisoned or suffer one of the other punishments mentioned below.

For the rich, however, fines were a definite advantage. They were a way of settling with the law, especially for acts of violence. By paying fines, the rich could escape other forms of punishment for almost any offence except murder and treason.

Whipping

More important during the eighteenth century was whipping. This could be done privately in a prison, or in public by the hangman. Most often it was imposed for petty theft. Whipping posts or the back of a cart were normally used. The criminal would be stripped to the waist and whipped 'until his back be bloody'. This punishment might also be given to women. The number of strokes was rarely specified and the carts might be drawn at varying speeds. This type of punishment was inflicted on commoners but not on aristocrats.

The pillory

The third and most traditional method was the use of the pillory, already described on page 26. This punishment was much more dangerous than it seems to us now. The offender might well be attacked by angry crowds, especially if the punishment was for an offence against a child. More often people were pilloried for cheating at cards or for petty fraud, or at the end of a whipping. The strength of the public's reaction can be seen in the case of a man pilloried at Cheapside, London in 1762:

Source 1

Gentleman's Magazine, 1762.

The populace fell upon the wretch, tore off his coat, waistcoat, shirt, hat, wig and breeches, and then pelted and whipped him till he had scarcely any signs of life left; he was then pulled off the pillory, but hung by his arms till he was set up again and stood in that naked condition, covered with mud, till the hour was out, and then was carried back to Newgate.

Some criminals who were pilloried did not survive at all. In some cases the law imposed an extra punishment of mutilation; an ear might be cut off while the victim's head was placed in the pillory.

Questions

1 When and why are fines used today? How does this differ from the use of fines in the eighteenth century?

2 Why were aristocrats not whipped? How would commoners have regarded this?

3 'The most important reason for pillorying was retribution.' Do you agree with this?

4 Why did so many people attend whippings and punishment by pillory? Would they do so today if these punishments were reintroduced?

6.1 The growth of the police

So far we have said very little about the officials responsible for keeping law and order. This is because there were very few developments before the nineteenth century. It was only then that a professional police force was finally set up.

Source 1

A watchman in Elizabethan times.

How did a police force develop?

Before 1829

Before the nineteenth century the enforcement of law and order in England and Wales was based on practices going back to the Middle Ages. In overall charge were the Justices of the Peace (J.P.s), appointed by the Crown from 1361 onwards. They were helped by constables, whose origins went back to Norman times. In turn, the constables were backed up by watchmen, who first appeared after the Statute of Winchester (1285). James I tried to introduce J.P.s into Scotland during the seventeenth century, but without much success.

As Britain's population gradually increased, and with it the number of crimes committed, other law enforcement officials were added. 'Bow Street runners' were appointed in London by the Bow Street magistrates, and the Thames river police were set up in 1800. Even so, whenever there were any serious disturbances in London, the government had to call upon the army. The J.P.s outside London depended on the 'yeomanry' and 'militia' to keep the peace.

The need for change

At the beginning of the nineteenth century, law and order was under constant threat.

Source 2

T. Bunyan's summary of the position reached in London's policing by the late 1820s, *The History of the Political Police in Britain*, (1976).

By the late 1820s London, a city with nearly one and a half million people, was policed by four hundred and fifty constables attached to magistrates' courts and some four thousand watchmen.

The memory of the Gordon riots (see pages 49–50) was still strong. There was also a steady stream of disturbances which included the Luddite riots, the Spa Fields riots, the Derbyshire insurrection and the Cato Street conspiracy (see page 56). In 1819 the massacre in St Peter's Fields in Manchester was a good example of how not to control a large crowd. It threw serious doubts on the use of the yeomanry for such purposes.

Added to these problems were the many instances of homicide, robbery, theft and burglary, all of which were increased as a result of the Industrial Revolution (see pages 41–45).

Beginning of the Metropolitan Police

The first major development was the formation of the Metropolitan Police

Force (MPF) in 1829 to cover the London area. This was done by the Home Secretary, Robert Peel, who believed that existing methods of maintaining law and order were not good enough.

Source 3

Peel's opinion in the 1820s.

> The country has entirely outgrown its police institutions.

Source 4

An 1830 cartoon of a Peeler.

MY OWN BLUE BELL, MY PRETTY BLUE BELL. &c. &c.

His Metropolitan Police Force was under the control of two commissioners. They had to report to the Home Secretary and were based at Scotland Yard. The force was divided into 17 divisions, each under a superintendent, served by 4 inspectors and 144 constables. London was now policed by 3,000 men altogether; they were soon nicknamed Peelers or Bobbies.

The uniform included a tall hat and long coats, both in dark blue. The intention was to make the new force look as unlike the army as possible. So they were also unarmed, except for truncheons.

At first there was much opposition to the new force. Peelers suffered violent attacks from members of the public. Gradually, however, fears were reduced and the force acquired a more positive image.

Source 5

The earliest known photograph of a Peeler.

Source 6

A broadsheet (poster) opposing the Metropolitan Police Force, 10 November 1830.

Peel's Police,
RAW LOBSTERS,
Blue Devils,

Or by whatever other appropriate Name they may be known.

Notice is hereby given,

That a Subscription has been entered into, to supply the **PEOPLE** with **STAVES** of a superior Effect, either for Defence or Punishment, which will be in readiness to be gratuitously distributed whenever a similar unprovoked, and therefore unmanly and blood-thirsty Attack, be again made upon Englishmen, by a Force unknown to the British Constitution, and called into existence by a Parliament illegally constituted, legislating for their individual interests, consequently in opposition to the Public good.

———ooo———

" Put not your trust in Princes."—DAVID.

" Help yourself, and Heaven will help you."—FRENCH MOTTO.

———

Eliz. Soulby, Printer, 91, Gracechurch Street.

Source 7

Punch magazine, 1851.

It is evident that the police are beginning to take their place in the affections of the people … that the soldiers used to occupy.

Early achievements of the force were mixed. On the one hand, recruits were often of poor quality and many were sacked for drunkenness. On the other hand, an 1830s writer argued that in one way the force had a very positive effect.

Source 8

J. Grant, *Sketches in London*, (1838).

diminution Reduction.
institution Formation.

I have said that there has been a great diminution in the amount of crime committed in London, since the institution of the new police. The great organisations of criminals have been broken up and scattered in all directions.

Grant was exaggerating when he referred to the collapse of the gangs but he was correct to point out that many criminals shifted their activities to outside London, into the boroughs and counties.

Extension of the police force

Peel's reforms applied only to London. Crime, of course, affected the whole country, so it was very important to take the same kinds of action to reform the boroughs and counties.

The first of the measures taken was the Municipal Corporations Act of 1835. This let boroughs set up watch committees to control a police force. The counties were brought into the new network by the 1839 County Police Act. Unfortunately the whole process was very patchy. The 1835 and 1839 Acts provided 'enabling' rather than 'compulsory' powers. This means that boroughs and counties could set up police forces if they wished; some, however, chose not to do so. These differences were set right by the 1856 County Borough Police Act, which made it compulsory for all counties and boroughs to set up a police force.

However, there was a further problem. The forces were very different in size and efficiency. Attempts had already been made to base all police forces on the unit of the county, but this had been fiercely resisted by the boroughs. There were no real changes in size and organisation of the police for another century (see page 105 for the next step).

Functions of the police

The most important function of the police was, of course, the control of crime. A Detective Department was established at Scotland Yard for the Metropolitan Police in 1842. Communications were speeded up by the use of telegraph from 1867, and the Criminal Investigation Department (CID) was set up in 1878. Records were not yet centralised in London, but were kept instead at each police station in the London area. Scotland Yard only kept details of the most notorious criminals.

Another function was the control of civil disturbances and riots. The new local police forces were normally used instead of the army and yeomanry. Most of them were competent, although it is worth noting that there was a fall in the number of civil disturbances between 1850 and 1900. Perhaps, therefore, the new forces were not yet fully tested.

Conditions in the police force

One of the major problems confronting the police forces in the nineteenth century was the lack of status and prestige given to them. A constable earned 29s. 6d. (just under £1.50) per week in 1876. Life as a police constable, in either the borough or the county police forces, was hard. Up to twelve hours per day would be spent patrolling on foot, although bicycles were provided after 1890. Whistles were used to summon help when needed.

Questions

1   The history of the nineteenth century police force shows how an improvement sometimes led to problems elsewhere. Give some examples of this.

2   Compare Sources 6 and 7 on police popularity. How reliable and useful would each one be? How would you explain the difference between them?

3   The modern police force has cars, motorcycles, telephones, radios and computerised records. What were the equivalent facilities for the nineteenth century police force?

4   Sherlock Holmes was a famous detective in late nineteenth century fiction. Why was he not portrayed as a member of the police force?

Part 3: Since 1900

A suffragette march, 1910

The twentieth century brought a large increase in crime. Unit 7 looks at the changing patterns of personal violence, theft, and vandalism, and deals with something entirely new: computer crimes. Unit 8 covers the wide range of protest seen during the twentieth century. This includes the active protest of demonstrators and marchers, the passive protest of conscientious objectors, the inner-city riots, and the more deliberate violence of terrorism.

Major changes have taken place since 1900 in policing and in the types of punishment used. These are examined in Unit 9.

Unit 7 · Crimes against property and the person

7.1 Violence and hooliganism

What types of violence?

The twentieth century has seen a steady rise in violence committed against the person. This section deals with homicide, violence within the family, gang hooliganism, and football violence.

Homicide

As in earlier periods, a distinction continues to be made between murder and manslaughter. It is even more common than before for such killings to take place within the family.

Source 1

Who are the main victims? Lord Windlesham's analysis, (1984).

It is remarkable to find that so many murders are first-time offenders who already knew the victim. In no less than three-quarters of all murder convictions, the victim and the offender had an existing relationship, whether living under the same roof or knowing one another less intimately.

Murders with a sexual motive are often the most sensational. They can involve serial killers like Peter Sutcliffe, the Yorkshire Ripper, and Denis Nilson. As in the nineteenth century, they are given heavy press coverage.

Most distressing is the abduction and murder of young children. It is, however, not known whether instances of this have increased since the beginning of the century or whether they are simply reported in more detail by the press.

Finally, murder is frequently committed during the course of other crimes, especially robbery. This may well involve the killing of a newsagent, or a security guard, or a policeman.

Violence within the family

More cases of violence within the family have come before the courts during the past three decades. There are two reasons for this. One is that more women have come forward to make complaints. The other is that the levels of violence against married women, which were once considered normal, are no longer socially or legally acceptable.

Violence against children is, however, more difficult to detect, because many families still accept the need for some form of beating for children, even if not for wives. Some European countries, like Sweden and the Netherlands, have made it illegal for parents to inflict corporal punishment on their children. It remains to be seen whether Britain eventually follows their example.

Gang hooliganism

Since 1945 there have been waves of youth groups which have involved organised violence. During the 1950s many people feared the Teddy Boys and Teds. They were so called because they imitated Edwardian fashions in clothes: they wore drainpipe trousers, long jackets, thick-soled shoes and had a duck-tail hairstyle. They were often involved in vandalism and street fights. They were replaced during the 1960s by the Mods and Rockers. These were deadly enemies of each other, and seaside resorts like Brighton and Southend saw some serious gang-fighting between them.

Still more violent were the Skinheads.

Source 2

A description of Skinheads from *New Society* magazine by Ian Walker (26 June 1980).

> Skinheads first arrived in the late 1960s. It was a sort of male working class backlash against mods grown too effeminate and arty.

They were also violently pro-British, pro-white, and racist. Their main targets were the immigrant population of the British cities. Worst affected were Asian Muslims like Pakistanis and Bangladeshis, but also highly vulnerable were Indians and people of Afro-Caribbean origin. Many Skinheads joined extreme right-wing parties like the National Front and took part in marches through parts of the inner cities inhabited by ethnic minorities.

Skinheads have also been closely associated with football violence. According to Ian Walker:

Source 2

continued

> Football fans discovered a style. I remember 4,000 Manchester United Skinheads on the terraces at Elland Road, Leeds, in 1968. They all wore bleached Levis, Dr Martens, a short scarf tied cravat-style, cropped hair. They looked like an army and, after the game, went into action like one.

Football violence

Football violence is, however, a problem which goes beyond the Skinheads. It was common before 1914, until all league matches were stopped by the outbreak of war. Between 1919 and 1939 behaviour improved, and it remained generally good between 1945 and 1957. Then football hooliganism rose sharply. Most violence is committed outside the grounds, either at stations, or the approach roads. It is often carried out by organised groups

Source 3

Violence at a football match.

of supporters who are well dressed. Examples include the Inter City Crew (supporting West Ham United), the Bushwackers (Millwall) and the Service Crew (Leeds United).

There have also been serious incidents abroad. Supermarkets have been ransacked, there has been loutish behaviour in the streets and bars, and local inhabitants have been threatened or assaulted. The worst incident occurred at Heysel stadium in Belgium on 29 May 1985, before the start of the European Cup Final between Liverpool and Juventus.

Source 4

David Waddington's description of the Heysel disaster (1992).

This happened when Juventus fans were chased out of an enclosure dominated by English supporters and, in the ensuing panic and rush to escape, a stadium wall collapsed, producing an appalling crush of bodies in which thirty-eight people (mostly Italian) died and 400 more were injured.

The blame was placed firmly on the hooligans by the inquiry into the disaster.

Source 5

The conclusion of the Popplewell Committee of Inquiry, (1986).

The final and most important lesson ... that if hooligans did not behave like hooligans at football matches there would be no such risk of injury.

What measures have been taken to discourage football hooliganism? The police ensure that rival fans are kept apart in the grounds and, where possible, use separate approach roads. There has also been an attempt by the police secretly to join football gangs, and to get to know how they operate, especially those going abroad. The football clubs have increased the amount of seating. They believe that most of the trouble inside the ground takes place on the terraces, where people stand. Some have also developed codes of conduct for their fans.

Source 6

An appeal by West Ham United football club to its fans.

An appeal to the "NORTH BANK BOYS"
So you have done it again. Not only did the behaviour of some of you at Ipswich make us feel thoroughly ashamed, but the result of your train-wrecking activities on the way home was seen by millions of people on Television. It must have filled them with utter disgust.

Why do you do it? If you consider yourselves to be supporters, then quite frankly, yours is the kind of support that both the game and this Club can well do without.

As we understand the term, a supporter is one who is proud of the Club and its record, proud of the team, and so proud of its reputation that he would do nothing to tarnish it.

Until you (dis)graced us with your presence two or three years ago, West Ham supporters were voted by British Railways as the best-behaved travellers in the game, and they still are – apart from you.

A very few of you are the ring-leaders, and we know who you are. So far you have exercised your "authority" in the very worst possible way, with your punch-ups, obscenities, and train-wrecking. Why not be different from the rest of your kind up and down the country? You could just as easily use your influence to bring this about.

Why cannot you follow the example of your seniors? Why cannot YOU be jealous of our reputation? Why cannot YOU become known as the best-behaved young supporters in the country? You would undoubtedly get just as much publicity – probably more!

Causes of hooliganism

Various reasons have been given for the growth of gang and football hooliganism.

1 The increase of violence on television and videos. A common argument is that young people become used to seeing violence and therefore do not really understand its full meaning.

2 The breakdown of family control. This is not a new complaint, as Source 7 shows.

Source 7

The Recorder of Bradford (a judge) on the decline of parental control, (1951).

Parents of this time, unfortunately, do not take sufficient care in bringing up their children. They expect somebody else to be responsible and it is a cause for great sorrow that 'Gone are the days of Queen Victoria'.

It is certainly true that the gang in many cases provides an alternative community, giving the security and stability which we normally associate with the family.

3 Deprivation (poor living conditions). This reason is hotly debated between, and even within, political parties. In 1946 the Conservative Party seemed to believe that people's behaviour was created by the conditions in which they lived.

Source 8

An extract from the publication *Youth Astray* (Conservative Political Centre, 1946).

hereditary Inherited from previous generations.

The misbehaviour of boys and girls is mainly the outcome of conditions, social, economic, and to some extent hereditary, for which they themselves cannot be blamed. The blame, for blame there is, rests upon society.

A decade later the same party was putting forward a different argument.

Source 9

An extract from the publication *The Responsible Society* (Conservative Political Centre, 1959).

propagate Spread.
malefactor Criminal.

We reject the notion, propagated by sincere but misguided idealists, that society shares the guilt of its criminals; that most malefactors are the victims of their environment.

To some observers the fault belonged to the welfare state, set up to help poor and unemployed people after the Second World War. A historian has argued that:

Source 10

Arthur Bryant in 1954 (in a foreword to a book on young people).

The drifting youth of the welfare state become the inevitable prey of the gang-leader or, at best, grow up to lead, despite all the material opportunities of our age, inert, stunted and purposeless lives.

This view would be rejected by a large number of politicians who still believe in the welfare state.

1 Why do most murderers know their victims?

2 Is the public today more obsessed with murder than it was in the nineteenth century? (See also pages 45–47.)

3 What are the similarities and differences between violent crime in the nineteenth century and today? (See also pages 41–47.)

4 Suggest reasons why the same political party produced sources as different as 8 and 9.

5 Is Source 10 what you would expect from a modern historian?

7.2   Burglary, theft and joyriding

Who commits theft, and where?

The average age of the criminal in Britain has got steadily lower when compared with that in 1900.

Source 1

The view of Lord Windlesham, a legal expert, (1984).

Youthful delinquents are responsible for a huge volume of property offences (the peak age for offending is fifteen), in complete contrast with the person of good character who commits one crime in a lifetime.

We might assume that the most vulnerable areas would be the wealthiest suburbs, but this is not the case. Most at risk are the poorest areas.

Source 2

Degree of risk of crime in different types of area. (Adapted from Lord Windlesham: *Responses to Crime*, Clarendon Press, Oxford, 1987.)

Type of area and housing	Crimes committed		
	Burglary percentage of households affected	Theft percentage of persons affected	Car crime percentage of owners affected
Low risk			
Agricultural	1	1.3	5
Retirement	3	1.1	6
Suburban	3	1.1	7
Modern, high income	3	0.9	8
Medium risk			
Better-off council	4	1.4	14
Poorer terraced	4	1.4	18
Less well-off council	4	1.4	15
High risk			
High status non-family	10	3.9	15
Multi-racial	10	4.3	26
Poorest council	12	3.3	21
National average	**4**	**1.4**	**11**

What types of theft?

Burglary

A considerable amount of burglary is now committed by young people in search of money or items they can sell to raise cash. This might be done to buy consumer articles, especially clothes and footwear. It might also be to feed a habit like drug-taking, particularly heroin, morphine, crack, ecstasy and LSD.

Source 3

Chief Superintendent Pearman in his book *The Hill*, (1989).

The drug culture encourages crime. People steal goods and cash to exchange for drugs.

Source 4

Stolen items which might be recovered by police.

Car theft

Crimes involving the theft of cars are normally of two types: theft for organised profit and theft for 'joyriding'.

1 Theft for profit

Most stolen cars are 'recycled'; they are usually given a new identity and sold by dishonest dealers. Engine numbers are changed and the milometer is altered to show a low mileage. Other alterations might include a paint respray and taking the registration number of a vehicle which has been scrapped. Police forces spend much of their time following up car thefts, and have introduced publicity campaigns urging people to install car alarms and steering wheel locks.

2 Joyriding

This is an activity confined almost entirely to the under-20 age group. Most joyriders are in fact under 16, some as young as 10. They have several motives. They may be looking for excitement, or they may enjoy the challenge of breaking into a car and starting an engine without a key. They may also be under pressure from friends. They may well, of course, be under the influence of alcohol or drugs.

Source 5

Howard Parker writing about joyriding, in *New Society* magazine, 5 September 1974.

It is still regarded with concern. This is because joyriding escapades involve extensive damage and often the total destruction of the vehicle taken, as well as damage to other property and possible injury to pedestrians.

Joyriding can also lead to major civil disturbances. In 1991 riots broke out on the Blackbird Leys estate in Oxford after police tried to stop the racing of stolen cars in the early morning.

Questions	
1	Discuss the possible reasons for the low, medium and high risk areas in Source 2.
2	Compare the reasons for burglary in 1990 with those in the eighteenth and nineteenth centuries. (See also pages 41–43.)
3	How does the theft of a car today differ from the theft of a horse in the eighteenth century? Are there any similarities between the two crimes? (See also pages 32–33.)

7.3   Destruction and vandalism

The term 'vandalism' comes from the Vandals, a barbarian tribe who caused great damage when they invaded the Roman Empire 1,500 years ago. Vandalism has become a major problem of twentieth century life, and is the most rapidly increasing of all crimes in this country. In 1950 about 0.5 million cases were recorded by the police; in 1989 this was 3.7 million, an increase of more than seven times.

The problem of vandalism

Types

Vandalism has been broken down into the following types:

1 'Ideological' vandalism. People commit acts of destruction to bring attention to a particular political or social problem which they believe should be solved.

2 'Acquisitive' vandalism. An object might be disturbed or broken for financial gain; valuable lead might be stolen from a roof, or coinboxes might be broken into.

3 'Tactical' vandalism. Some criminals cause destruction to catch the attention of authorities, while they then go on to commit a more serious crime elsewhere.

4 'Vindictive' vandalism. People settle grudges against other people, or show an act of defiance against authority.

5 'Play' vandalism. Vandalism results from high-spirited competition between individuals and groups, often in the form of a 'dare'.

Source 1 shows a list of specific acts of vandalism.

Why does it occur?

There has always been a debate on the causes of vandalism. On one side are those who blame the vandal's environment (living conditions). On the other side are those who place all the blame on the individual concerned.

Source 1

Acts of vandalism committed by schoolchildren in 1978. Percentages refer to the proportion of boys who admitted to having committed the specified act at least once in the previous six months.

1	Scratched desk at school	85%
2	Broken a bottle in the street	79%
3	Broken a window in an empty house	68%
4	Written on walls in the street	65%
5	Broken trees or flowers in a park	58%
6	Written on the seats or walls of buses	55%
7	Broken the glass in a street lamp	48%
8	Scratched a car or lorry	42%
9	Smashed things on a building site	40%
10	Broken a window in an occupied house	32%
11	Broken glass in a bus shelter	32%
12	Damaged park building	31%
13	Broken furniture at school	29%
14	Broken a window in a public toilet	29%
15	Broken a glass of a telephone kiosk	28%
16	Broken a car radio aerial	28%
17	Damaged the tyres of a car	28%
18	Broken a window at school	27%
19	Slashed bus seats	22%
20	Broken a seat in a public toilet	20%
21	Damaged telephone in a kiosk	20%
22	Put large objects on a railway line	19%
23	Broken a window in a club	16%
24	Slashed train seats	12%

The 'environmentalists' believe that vandalism is brought on by frustration. This is caused by a lack of recreation facilities, bad housing, large featureless blocks of flats, and poor education. Some sociologists believe that Britain has developed a large 'underclass', especially in the inner cities.

Douglas Hurd, Home Secretary in 1988, was not convinced by the environmental argument.

Source 2

Douglas Hurd speaking at a conference on vandalism in 1988.

We are not dealing here with some protest movement, whether against the government, police or society as a whole.

The press usually goes further in this direction. Here is a typical example.

Source 3

News of the World newspaper, 8 May 1966.

They are known as vandals. I call them potential murderers. They are the lads who wreck telephone boxes for the sheer hell of it, and so hold up emergency calls to doctors, hospitals and ambulance services.

Whether or not the environment has much to do with vandalism, drugs and alcohol certainly do. Alcohol is especially problematic, and there has been a massive spread of under-age drinking in Britain.

Source 4

Mary Tuck, *Drinking and Disorder*, (1989).

Going out to pubs is quite simply what young people do on a weekend evening, to meet others and to enjoy themselves ... Young people leave pubs en masse at the same hour, emerge on the streets still looking for further entertainment, cluster at fast-food outlets or at other gathering points and are at this point excitable tinder, ready for any spark....

Dealing with vandalism

How can vandalism be dealt with? There is a variety of options.

1 The law. The most recent law concerning damage is the 1971 Act of Parliament.

At present a fine is the most commonly used form of punishment and is applied to 65% of those found guilty. Many people in society want tougher sentences for vandals, including time to be spent in detention centres, or corporal punishment. There have even been suggestions that the stocks and pillory should be brought back.

2 Social responsibility. Some argue that the community should be made more responsible for its young people and for its property. People can also be made more aware and observant through schemes like the Neighbourhood Watch (see page 106).

3 More facilities. If some vandalism is caused by boredom, then providing improved recreation facilities and adventure playgrounds for younger children should help.

4 Education and publicity. Local authorities, police forces and schools sometimes become involved in a campaign to prevent vandalism. The City of Birmingham, for example, launched a 'Stop Vandalism Week' in 1967.

Source 5

The first page of the 1971 Criminal Damage Act of Parliament.

Criminal Damage Act 1971   c. 48   1

ELIZABETH II

1971 CHAPTER 48

An Act to revise the law of England and Wales as to offences of damage to property, and to repeal or amend as respects the United Kingdom certain enactments relating to such offences; and for connected purposes.   [14th July 1971]

Be it enacted by the Queen's most Excellent Majesty by, and with the advice and consent of the Lords Spiritual and Temporal, and Commons, in this present Parliament assembled, and by the authority of the same, as follows:—

1.—(1) A person who without lawful excuse destroys or damages any property belonging to another intending to destroy or damage any such property or being reckless as to whether any such property would be destroyed or damaged shall be guilty of an offence.   *Destroying or damaging property.*

(2) A person who without lawful excuse destroys or damages any property, whether belonging to himself or another—

(a) intending to destroy or damage any property or being reckless as to whether any property would be destroyed or damaged ; and

(b) intending by the destruction or damage to endanger the life of another or being reckless as to whether the life of another would be thereby endangered ;

shall be guilty of an offence.

(3) An offence committed under this section by destroying or damaging property by fire shall be charged as arson.

2. A person who without lawful excuse makes to another a threat, intending that that other would fear it would be carried out,—   *Threats to destroy or damage property.*

(a) to destroy or damage any property belonging to that other or a third person ; or

---

IF YOU LEND A HAND WE CAN

STOP vandalism

LEND A HAND & STOP THE VANDALS

If you are a:

RATEPAYER — Do YOU realise that it costs over £50,000 of YOUR MONEY each year to make good the damage done by vandals to Corporation property alone. The cost to everyone in the City is far greater, and in the long run YOU PAY.

PROPERTY OWNER — We ask that YOU take all precautions to protect your property and not to place temptation in the path of a potential vandal. If YOU own any dilapidated buildings which serve no useful purpose, please have them demolished. Remember that even if YOU are insured YOU PAY in increased premiums and inconvenience.

PARENT — Please do everything YOU can to impress on your children how futile it is to wreck other people's property. Please help them to use their leisure time profitably. Don't blame the authorities if they are caught and punished, because in the end YOU PAY.

YOUNG PERSON — Please think before YOU wreck something. Think about how much more fun it may give YOU and others if YOU help to protect it rather than break it. Even if YOU are not caught, it is YOUR parents who will PAY for the damage, and if YOU are caught YOU *will* PAY.

TEACHER — Please impress on every member of your class how silly it is to destroy the things which are provided to make their lives more pleasant.

YOUTH WORKER — Please try to widen your net and give as many young people as possible the opportunities which your organisation is able to give them.

VANDAL — Someone will be watching YOU — and have YOU thought that if YOU wreck a public telephone — it may be YOUR MOTHER who wants a doctor in an emergency.

YOU may not always be able to stop an act of vandalism yourself, but YOU can dial 999 — because it does concern YOU

Remember if we don't stop vandalism

you will pay

Source 6   A display card from Birmingham's 'Stop Vandalism Week', January 1967.

Source 7

Posters aimed at increasing parental responsibility.

5 'Hardening' targets. This means making vandalism more difficult by improving security, supervising playgrounds and providing stronger fittings within buildings used by the public. Telephone boxes have been redesigned and there have been experiments with different types of wall coverings to protect against graffiti.

Above all, public facilities are now more often designed so that they are in the open and easily seen. Unfortunately, the vandal's life has been made easier by one recent development, and we see the results of it every day.

Source 8

The effect of aerosol spray paints, according to a sociologist, Stanley Cohen.

Aerosol sprays are much quicker and easier to apply than paint, and fairly long slogans can be sprayed … in a matter of seconds. This decreases the chances of detection even in busy public settings and allows a number of offences to be committed in a short time.

Questions

1 Under which of the five types of vandalism would you put each of the offences listed in Source 1? (Some of these offences may involve more than one type of vandalism.)

2 Explain to an eighteenth century Londoner the meaning and causes of twentieth century vandalism.

3 Read carefully through the section on 'Dealing with vandalism'. Divide the class into two groups. One group should think of as many objections as possible to the measures listed in the section. The other group should try to provide answers to these objections.

4 How effective is Source 6 as a display card against vandalism? Comment on
a its arguments
b the people it is most likely to influence.

5 What are the similarities and differences between the posters in Source 7? Which do you consider the more effective?

7.4 Computer crime

Whole new areas of crime have been opened up, especially since 1970, by the spectacular advances made in computer technology. The computer is an attractive target for the expert criminal. It has complex functions, which most people do not fully understand. It operates at high speed, making checking difficult. Also, most faults which are discovered can be explained as 'computer error', rather than the deliberate interference of an outsider.

This section offers a collection of views from experts on a problem which is likely to become more and more important in the future.

What is computer crime?

Source 1

The definition of computer crime by author Steven Mandell, (1990).

perpetrate Carry out.
hardware Mechanical and electronic parts of computers.
software Computer discs and tapes.

Computer crime ... consists of two kinds of activity:
a the use of a computer to perpetrate acts of deceit, theft or concealment that are intended to provide financial, business-related, property, or service advantages; and
b threats to the computer itself, such as theft of hardware or software, sabotage, and demands for ransom.

These two types, crimes *using* computers and crimes *against* computers, are the basis for the rest of this section.

Crimes using computers

Some crimes involve the use of the computer as a friendly agent. The type of crime is traditional: theft, fraud, or blackmail; but the method is modern.

1 Theft of computer time

Computers are adaptable machines, capable of carrying out a variety of functions. The largest are often shared between users, who all have their own separate security code. Some users succeed in stealing others' allocated time by accessing (finding out and using) their codes. There are other methods of theft, such as 'piggybacking'.

Source 2

'Piggybacking', explained by Steven Mandell, (1990).

By 'piggybacking' into a legitimate user's line, one can have free use of the user's privileges whenever the line is not being used by the authorised party.

2 Financial fraud

There are three types of financial fraud, all made possible by computerised accounts. One is the re-routing of funds, which literally disappear from one account, and then re-appear in another. In the second type, funds can be taken out of accounts by cheques, produced by instructions which get round the computer's security system. The third type is known as the 'round off fraud'. This means the removal of the fractions of a penny (or cent in America) which are caused by changes in the interest rate. These fractions can eventually add up to a sizable amount in a separate account.

In all these types of fraud, banks are especially at risk.

Source 3

Bank robbery via computers, explained by author Leslie D. Ball, (1985).

Banks often figure in computer crimes because of the increasing use of electronic funds transfer symbols, which move huge sums of money among banks with electronic symbols as the only record. This system replaces the personal signatures that once accompanied every banking transaction code, a series of unique digits identifying any bank official who can authorise money transfers. Large numbers of financial transactions can be made quickly and at less expense using such a system, but trouble brews if the codes fall into the wrong hands.

3 Accessing confidential programmes

Some computer criminals concentrate on stealing valuable records. They might hope to gain detailed knowledge of another company's secrets or a distribution list which might otherwise take many months to compile. In some cases, personal records might be opened up, giving opportunities for blackmail.

Crimes against computers

We have seen how the criminal can use the computer as an accomplice. Sometimes, however, the computer is itself the victim. The most common crime against computers is sabotage. This involves deliberate damage to hardware or software.

Sometimes the aim of sabotage is total destruction. In the early days of computers there were fears that jobs would be lost and some saboteurs were compared with the Luddites. Alternatively, there might be political activists who object to the policies of a particular company and destroy its machines to show this. Personal revenge might also be a motive.

Source 4

A motive for sabotage explained by Steven Mandell, (1990).

One fired employee simply walked through the data storage area with an electromagnet, thereby erasing valuable company records.

The most recent form of sabotage is the deliberate creation of 'misinformation' on a computer disc. When introduced into the computer this acts as a 'virus', destroying existing programs and records.

Sometimes the criminal aims at creating an error which is less drastic than a virus. This is called a 'trapdoor'.

Source 5

The 'trapdoor' technique explained by author Murray Laver, (1991).

In a technique known as 'trapdoor and patch' an unscrupulous skilled programmer conceals ... a sequence of instructions (the patch) beneath a 'trapdoor' inserted into an application program. Such a trapdoor consists of a conditional jump instruction that would be passed over unnoticed in normal use. Only when the criminal injects into the input data a pre-arranged code group that could not occur in the ordinary course, is the branching condition met, the trapdoor opened and the patch entered and obeyed.

There are two main reasons for doing this. One is to create extra work (and paid overtime) whenever the criminal wants it. The other is to hide certain financial information to reduce the amount of tax and VAT to be paid.

Who commits computer crimes?

According to another expert, individuals are the main offenders.

Source 6

An analysis by R. Kling, (1991).

Usually these are frauds or thefts in which isolated individuals abuse organisations, rather than cases in which organisations abuse their clients in the course of doing relatively routine business.

Persons carrying out these crimes are normally 'white collar' employees, mainly men in their twenties, with considerable knowledge and expertise.

Some offenders are known as 'hackers', many of whom are pupils or students. They become totally obsessed with computers. Experiments become pranks, then pranks become criminal acts.

Source 7

The motive of the 'hacker', according to Murray Laver, (1991).

I.T. Information technology.

One group with specialist knowledge and a nickname are the 'hackers'. Some of them are amateurs, but all are obsessed with the intellectual challenge of computing. The growth of I.T. networks accessible over public telephone services has provided hackers with an irresistible target, and they are prepared to devote a great many hours to solving the fascinating puzzle of how to break into a commercial or governmental system.

This theme has been used in many feature films, like 'War Games', and television dramas.

Questions

1 Conduct an interview between a company representative who is about to install a computer system, and an expert pointing out possible problems of security.

2 Discuss the statement: 'Computer hackers should not be seen as criminals in the same way as those who use computers to defraud (cheat or swindle)'.

3 Discuss the statement: 'Scrooge's money would be more at risk in a computerised account than in a bank vault.'

4 Is computer crime less serious than violent crime?

Unit 8 · Challenges to authority

8.1 Active protest: marches and demonstrations

At times people feel they have to protest against existing laws or conditions by going on demonstrations and marches. In the twentieth century there has been a wide variety. Source 1 shows a few examples.

Source 1

Some examples of active protest since 1900.

Protesters	Motivation	Period
Suffragettes	To demand a specific right: women's right to vote	pre-1914
Hunger marches	To protest against social conditions	1930s
Blackshirt parades	To set up a fascist state	1930s
CND, anti-Vietnam War protests, anti-Poll Tax protests	To force the government to give up a specific policy	1960s–1990s

Women's suffrage

Women's organisations were generally agreed that women had the right to vote, but they were divided over tactics for achieving it. The more moderate National Union of Women's Suffrage Societies (NUWSS) wanted to have legal demonstrations only. Several great marches were held before the outbreak of the First World War. In June 1908, for example, 13,000 marched from the Embankment to the Albert Hall in London, carrying banners with the slogan 'Votes for Women'.

More drastic measures were taken by the Women's Social and Political Union (WSPU). These women agreed to break the law to achieve their aims. They caused obstruction by chaining themselves to railings, they set fire to letter boxes, and they broke windows in the houses of politicians known to be against women's suffrage. Their leader, Emmeline Pankhurst, argued that there was no other way to make their feelings known.

Source 2

Emmeline Pankhurst justifying a policy of protest in Bow Street magistrate's court, 1908.

We have tried every way. We have presented larger petitions than were ever presented before for any other reform, we have succeeded in holding greater public meetings than men have ever held for any reform. We have faced hostile mobs at street corners ... If you had the power to send us to prison, not for six months but for six years, or for the whole of our lives, the government must not think that they can stop this agitation. It will go on. We are going to win.

When the suffragettes were arrested they went on hunger strike. The authorities treated this as attempted suicide, then seen as a crime, and therefore started to force-feed the women.

Women were given the vote in the Representation of the People Act of 1918, although the government was quick to claim that this was a reward for women's services in the war, and not a response to pressure.

Unemployment marches of the 1930s

Marches were held all over the country during the period after 1929, mainly against the high levels of unemployment and decreases in dole money. The most spectacular were the marches to London from a number of different cities. The best known example was the Jarrow Crusade which took place in October 1936, as a protest against ship-building job losses.

The government, however, refused to be influenced by any of the marches.

Source 3

The Jarrow Crusade. Jarrow is near Newcastle, so the march was over 250 miles long.

Source 4

The Prime Minister, Stanley Baldwin, in a debate in Parliament, (published in *The Times*, 15 October 1936).

Processions to London cannot claim to have any constitutional influence on policy. Ministers have, therefore, decided that encouragement cannot be given to such marches, whatever their particular purpose, and ministers cannot consent to receive any deputation of marchers, although of course, they are always prepared to meet any Members of Parliament.

deputation A group sent to speak for a larger set of people.

Many of the marches and demonstrations were organised by the National Unemployed Workers' Movement (NUWM), which the government regarded as having threatening, communist views. There was also opposition from other people:

Source 5

The Times, 28 October 1932.

Is there to be no limit to the right of the workless to hamper the workers? The evil will grow if it is not checked. There are plenty of ways in which legitimate discontent may be rationally expressed.

checked Stopped.

The government did take some measures to deal with the problems of recession and unemployment, but it always stated that these measures were nothing to do with pressures from demonstrators and marchers.

The Fascist marches of the 1930s

The British Union of Fascists (BUF) was set up by Sir Oswald Mosley. He intended Britain to become a Fascist state similar to Italy, which was being led by Mussolini, a man he greatly admired. The total number of members, called 'Blackshirts', reached 20,000 by 1934. There were many meetings and rallies; the most famous was held at Olympia in London, on 7 June 1934.

Source 6

A Conservative M.P.'s description of the Olympia meeting (Geoffrey Lloyd's letter to the *Yorkshire Post* newspaper).

I was appalled by the brutal conduct of the Fascists ... I saw with my own eyes case after case of single interrupters being attacked by ten to twenty Fascists. Again and again, as five or six Blackshirts carried out an interrupter by arms and legs, several other Blackshirts were engaged in kicking and hitting his helpless body ... It was a deeply shocking scene for an Englishman to see in London. The Blackshirts behaved like bullies and cads.

The Blackshirts targeted the Jews as the reason for Britain's difficulties. They were also strongly against people with left-wing views. They marched through London to provoke reactions, and there were clashes with other groups, including the NUWM, which organised anti-Fascist demonstrations. Right- and left-wing groups therefore aggravated and stirred up violence against each other.

Source 7

Fascist and anti-Fascist meetings in London 1936–7.

Date	Number of meetings	
	Fascist	Anti-Fascist
December 1936	61	70
January 1937	103	141
February 1937	222	184

The Fascist movement began to decline from 1937. This was partly because of government measures such as the 1936 Public Order Act (which banned the wearing of para-military uniforms), and partly because the British public were becoming more aware of the dangers of fascism in Europe. When war broke out with Germany, Mosley was imprisoned and his movement collapsed.

Anti-government demonstrations since 1955

Since the mid-1950s three issues have caused much public campaigning and protest. These are the government's policy on nuclear weapons, its decision to support American involvement in the Vietnam War, and its introduction of the poll tax.

CND

The Campaign for Nuclear Disarmament (CND) was set up to persuade the government not to rely on nuclear arms as a deterrent. During the 1950s and 1960s the main activity was by public demonstrations. The Aldermaston march is a famous example.

During the 1970s and 1980s the strategy changed to surrounding key US air bases which kept bombers armed with nuclear weapons. One example was Greenham Common. Here, most of the protestors were women who acted as a human barrier against military supplies entering the base. There were many clashes with police, who tried to move the women when they were blocking gates. They were sometimes accused of being too heavy-handed.

Source 8

The Aldermaston march.

Source 9

The women of Greenham Common.

After forty years, CND had still not achieved its original objective, in three ways. Firstly, Britain had remained a nuclear power. Secondly, the Labour Party, which once supported CND, changed its mind. Thirdly, the United States continued to have nuclear bombers based in Britain. On the other hand, CND did much to inform the public about the terrible dangers of nuclear war.

The Vietnam demonstrations

When the British governments of the 1960s supported the US involvement against the Communists in Vietnam, there were many protests, especially from students. A crowd assembled outside the US embassy in Grosvenor Square, London in October 1967, and there were violent clashes between demonstrators and police. Further marches took place in March the following year. These were organised by the Vietnam Solidarity Campaign (VSC).

There was a contrast between the activities of the CND and the VSC. The CND were highly organised and tried to avoid disruption. The VSC marches, on the other hand, aimed at creating disruption. The VSC also saw its objective fulfilled. The war in Vietnam ended in 1975, although this was not *directly* because of the campaigns of the late 1960s.

Poll tax riots

Sometimes disturbances occur in response to a specific law. Particularly unpopular was the community charge, or poll tax, introduced by the government in the late 1980s to replace council rates. This was opposed almost immediately by students in many universities and colleges. In addition, large numbers of people refused to pay the charge. Finally, in March 1990 a demonstration was held in Trafalgar Square. This turned into violence as cars were overturned and set on fire. There was some looting in the West End of London as the crowd eventually moved off.

All three main political parties blamed people with extreme political views for the riots (especially 'anarchists' and the Socialist Workers Party). Shortly afterwards, however, the Government decided to withdraw the poll tax. It claimed that pressure from the campaigners was nothing to do with the decision, but many people thought otherwise.

Questions

1. Which of the protests in this section did the government of the day consider the most dangerous?

2. List the protests in this section in order of their eventual success. Do this in the form of a chart with headings: 'Protest', 'Government reaction' and 'Result/effect'. Give reasons for your choice.

3. Which of the protests do you think was *most* justifiable and which was *least* justifiable? Give reasons.

4. How much can be worked out from Sources 8 and 9 about the two different strategies used by CND?

8.2 Passive protest: conscientious objectors

One form of protest during the twentieth century was more peaceful; in fact it was a protest against violence itself.

Conscientious objectors (COs) refused to take part in the organised violence of war for strongly felt reasons. They were pacifists who were put in the position of having to decide whether or not to disobey an order to fight.

This was never a problem until the twentieth century, because all wars had been fought by professional armies, recruited from volunteers. Anyone objecting to war therefore simply avoided joining up. This choice ended during the two periods of total war, 1914–18 and 1939–45, when compulsory service in the army was introduced. Suddenly, it was no longer possible not to fight; to refuse to serve in the army became an act of defiance, even a crime.

Some conscientious objectors refused to do anything which might contribute to the war effort. Others were less extreme. They did not try to stop the war itself, but argued that it is morally wrong for a government to force citizens to fight. There might also be some way in which a CO could help in a non-combatant (non-fighting) role.

How has the state's attitude to conscientious objectors changed?

Source 1

A recruiting poster from the First World War.

Daddy, what did YOU do in the Great War?

Source 2

A poster announcing the procedures to get a certificate of exemption during the First World War.

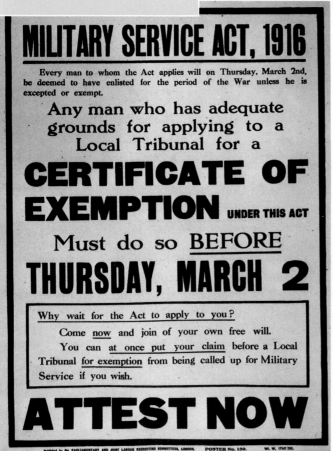

A government urgently needs people to fight during wars. Each citizen is required to contribute to the state's continued existence. In normal times this means co-operating with authorities and paying taxes. In emergencies it means being prepared to make sacrifices, from which no one should be exempt.

During the First World War the government adopted a tough policy, which eased up a little in the Second World War. Public attitudes, however, remained constant in both World Wars, and conscientious objectors had a very hard time.

First World War

Between 1914 and 1916 the government relied on volunteers to fight, although more and more pressure was placed on men to join the army.

Then, in May 1916, conscription was introduced for men between 18 and 41, and the upper age limit was later increased to 51. Exemption was possible in certain cases, as shown in Source 2.

During the First World War conscientious objection was very difficult. COs were interviewed by tribunals, and some were offered alternative work for the War effort. However, they were widely accused of being cowards by the public; some were attacked, and most were shut out from society. About 30% of the total number were imprisoned by the authorities, while many others eventually obeyed the order to fight. Grudges lasted until well after the War. For example, conscientious objectors were not allowed to vote until 1923.

Second World War

By the time of the Second World War official attitudes had changed. Partly responsible for this new view was Neville Chamberlain, Prime Minister at the time when conscription was brought back.

Source 3

Neville Chamberlain introducing the 1939 Act restoring conscription.

Where scruples are conscientiously held we desire that they should be respected and that there should be no persecution of those who hold them.

When Winston Churchill replaced Chamberlain as Prime Minister in 1940, he had the same view; he believed that any persecution would be 'odious to the British people'.

Tribunals were set up to examine the reasons why some people did not want to be conscripted. They sent men to prison only as a last resort. Conscientious objectors were given different types of work. Some remained at home in agriculture or industry, keeping their original jobs if these were considered valuable for the War effort. Others served as non-combatants in the forces, driving ambulances or carrying out other medical work.

Source 4

The number of conscientious objectors in the Second World War.

Total claiming exemption	59,192
Those granted unconditional exemption	3,577
Those exempted but given work	28,720
Those given non-combatant work in the forces	14,691
Those refused exemption	12,204

Some organisations co-operated with the government; these included the Central Board for Conscientious Objectors, and the Society of Friends, a much older religious group. Others, however, went further than just refusing to fight. The Peace Pledge Union tried to persuade others not to do so, but even these activities were not prosecuted.

Source 5

A court case involving Peace Pledge Union objectors, from Angus Calder's book *The People's War, Britain 1939–1945*, (1969).

Six Peace Pledge Union organisers were on trial at Bow Street police court for putting up a poster which said 'War will cease when men refuse to fight. What are YOU doing about it?'. The magistrate dismissed the case, saying, 'This is a free country. We are fighting to keep it a free country, as I understand it'.

Unfortunately, the British people were less tolerant than the authorities. Many conscientious objectors were sacked from their jobs and some were openly attacked. All were accused of cowardice or treason.

Class activity

■ Choose four members of the class to draw up a personality profile (description) for each of four conscientious objectors. Then split the rest of the class into two tribunals, one for World War I, the other for World War II. The four conscientious objectors are interviewed in turn by the two tribunals. The tribunals then discuss the cases. What differences come out of these discussions? (The profile might include: name, background, reasons for being a conscientious objector, and so on.)

8.3 Riots in British cities

Source 1

The location of the main urban riots since 1900.

Source 1 provides a summary of the most important disturbances to have affected Britain's cities this century. Even a quick glance indicates that rioting has been a serious problem.

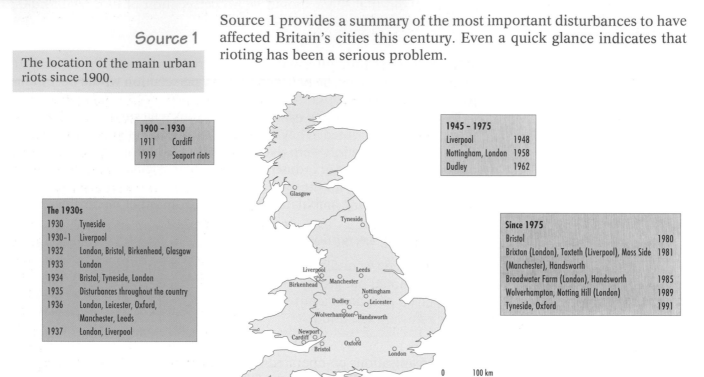

1900 – 1930

| 1911 | Cardiff |
| 1919 | Seaport riots |

1945 – 1975

Liverpool	1948
Nottingham, London	1958
Dudley	1962

The 1930s

1930	Tyneside
1930-1	Liverpool
1932	London, Bristol, Birkenhead, Glasgow
1933	London
1934	Bristol, Tyneside, London
1935	Disturbances throughout the country
1936	London, Leicester, Oxford, Manchester, Leeds
1937	London, Liverpool

Since 1975

Bristol	1980
Brixton (London), Toxteth (Liverpool), Moss Side (Manchester), Handsworth	1981
Broadwater Farm (London), Handsworth	1985
Wolverhampton, Notting Hill (London)	1989
Tyneside, Oxford	1991

0   100 km

When and where did riots occur?

1900–1930

Disturbances between 1900 and the 1970s were mainly by racist groups against immigrant communities. In 1911, for example, the Chinese people in Cardiff were attacked for allegedly not taking part in a strike by the National Seaman and Fireman's Union. More extensive were the seaport riots of 1919. These started in East London and spread to Liverpool, Newport, Cardiff, Tyneside and Glasgow. The targets were black seamen, who were accused of taking jobs and mixing with white women.

Source 2

Mosley's Fascists in the 1930s.

The 1930s

There were so many disturbances in the 1930s, that this period came to be known as the 'Devil's Decade'. Some involved religious groups, for example, Orangemen (Protestants) and Catholics in Liverpool in 1931, and in Glasgow in 1932. The worst unrest, however, involved Mosley's Fascists (see page 93), who stirred up trouble against two opponents. One set of opponents was the hunger marchers, the other set was racial minorities, especially Jews. Every year from 1931 to 1939 there was serious fighting (see Source 1). The worst was 1936, when the government introduced the Public Order Act. This, and the outbreak of the Second World War, gradually brought the problem under control.

1945–1975

After the War, disturbances returned to the streets of Britain. Again, most were racial. In Liverpool in 1948, black clubs were attacked by crowds, and street battles followed. There were also clashes between whites and blacks in the city centre of Nottingham in 1958. In the same year, London Teddy Boys attacked black individuals and homes. In 1962, there were riots lasting over four nights in Dudley, as the police tried to prevent white gangs from invading black areas.

Since 1975

During the late 1970s and the 1980s the pattern of rioting began to change. Instead of whites assaulting immigrants, with the police trying to restore order, the police themselves became the target. They were attacked mainly by youths in the inner cities, some white, the majority Afro-Caribbean.

The first real sign of this pattern came in the Notting Hill carnivals of 1976 and 1977, which ended in the smashing of windows and the stoning of police vehicles. Then, in 1980, Britain seemed to explode in a series of major riots, worse than any since the 'Devil's Decade'.

The first two occurred in Bristol (1980) and Brixton in London (1981). Days after the Brixton riot, Liverpool was also having serious problems. A motorcyclist was pursued by police for a traffic offence. When a young black man tried to prevent him from being arrested the police called in more support, and a large crowd gathered. The riot spread through the Toxteth area, especially Upper Parliament Street. Buildings were burned, and 214 police vehicles damaged. CS gas (tear gas) was used for the first time on the British mainland. During the same summer Moss Side in Manchester and Handsworth in Birmingham also erupted.

1985 was another bad year. A riot was started in Handsworth by an argument between police and a black youth about a parking ticket. Three hours later over 40 buildings were on fire. Shortly afterwards, tragic events occurred on the Broadwater Farm housing estate in Tottenham, London. A black woman, Cynthia Jarrett, died during a police search of her house. In the riot which followed, police constable Keith Blakelock was killed. In 1989 there were further disturbances in Wolverhampton and Notting Hill, and in Tyneside and Oxford in 1991. The last of these happened when the police tried to stop the racing of stolen cars on the Blackbird Leys estate in the early hours of the morning.

Source 3

The Toxteth riots in 1981.

What caused the riots in the 1980s?

The riots of the 1980s have a particular theme in common: the confrontation between crowds and the police. Some very different theories have been suggested for this. Some people put the blame firmly on the rioters. Others say there were 'mitigating circumstances', or situations where the rioters were not completely at fault.

Explanations putting full blame on the rioters

1 Conspiracy

Source 4

The explanation given by the *Daily Express* newspaper for the Broadwater Farm riot, 8 October 1985.

The thugs who murdered policeman Keith Blakelock in the Tottenham riots acted on the orders of crazed left-wing extremists.

Street-fighting experts trained in Moscow and Libya were behind Britain's worst violence.

2 Villainy and evil

Ian Percival, M.P. for Southport, thought that the threat was:

Source 5

Sir Ian Percival's point of view, *Hansard*, the journal of Parliament, 23 October 1985.

A combination of sheer villainy on an unprecedented scale, exploiting every grievance, real or supposed, and a deliberate, skilled, organised and dedicated attack on our very way of life.

3 Mob excitement and weaknesses of human nature

Source 6

The Home Secretary in the House of Commons, *Hansard*, 23 October 1985.

The excitement of forming and belonging to a mob, the evident excitement of violence leading to the fearsome crimes that we have seen reported and the greed that leads to looting ... to explain all these things in terms of deprivation and suffering is to ignore some basic and ugly facts about human nature.

4 Lack of discipline

Source 7

The view of Mr Giles Shaw, Minister of State at the Home Office, *Hansard*, 23 October 1985.

In Britain today discipline is a dirty word. It has long since ebbed from millions of homes and it has been dragged from thousands of schools. The police stand as the main bastion of discipline and responsibility in our society.

5 Wilful obstruction of the police

Source 8

Sir Kenneth Newman, Chief Constable of the Metropolitan Police, from the journal *Police*, September 1983.

In many multi-ethnic areas police encounter not merely apathy and unhelpfulness when making enquiries or engaging in order maintenance, but outright hostility and obstruction. It is commonplace in some multi-ethnic areas for a policeman making a legitimate arrest ... to be surrounded by a hostile crowd bent on 'rescuing' the prisoner or interviewee.

6 Disruptive influences within minority ethnic groups

Source 9

Daily Mail newspaper, 5 October 1985.

Either they obey the laws of this land where they have taken up residence and accepted the full rights and responsibilities of citizenship, or they must expect the Fascist street agitators to call ever more boldly and with ever louder approval for them to 'go back from whence they come'.

Explanations of mitigating circumstances

Source 10

T. Jefferson and R. Grimshaw point out the negative effects of using the Special Patrol Group in Brixton, London.

blunderbuss An old type of gun, now used as a term to describe heavy-handed methods.

1 Heavy policing

What seemed to have happened was that the police campaign like a crude blunderbuss had directed its fire against general illegality and delinquency in Brixton, catching many with its blast and threatening innocents, without restraining the growth of the central problem. More than that, the hostility of black people to the police was a direct consequence of the police campaign, and was arguably increasing the difficulty of the police task.

2 Social deprivation

Source 11

John Fraser, M.P. for Norwood (which includes Brixton), documented in *Hansard*, 23 October 1985.

It is impossible to divorce the catastrophic cuts in housing, the catastrophic increase in unemployment and the catastrophic cuts in all sorts of services in the constituency and borough that I represent, from what has happened in that area.

3 Racial disadvantage

Source 12

Lord Scarman speaking about the importance of racial issues (1981).

Racial disadvantage is a fact of current British life. It was, I am equally sure, a significant factor in the causation of the Brixton disorders.

A combination of factors: the Scarman Report

Lord Scarman was appointed to be the head of a committee to examine the background of the Brixton riots in 1981. His 1981 report argued that the riot was due to a complex combination of factors. These included unemployment, social disadvantage, poor housing, racial discrimination, and the belief that the police were harassing black people.

Source 13

Lord Scarman's view (1981).

The police must carry some responsibility for the disorders ... The community and community leaders must take their share of the blame for ... distrust and mutual suspicion between the community and the police.

Questions

1 Use your local reference library. Find the relevant copy of *Keesing's Contemporary Archives*, and read the details of one specific riot since 1980.

2 Investigate this riot by thinking about the various reasons provided in this section.

3 List these reasons in what you think is their order of importance. Explain your decisions.

4 Compare the modern inner-city riots with the Gordon riots of 1780. What do they have in common, and what are their differences? (See also pages 49–50.)

8.4 Terrorism in Britain

What is terrorism?

Examples of terrorism

Reading the newspapers, it is easy to believe that the United Kingdom (which includes Northern Ireland) is more seriously affected by terrorism than any other country in Europe. In fact, during the 1970s and 1980s, there was a general increase in violence committed by terrorist groups all over Europe, as Source 1 shows.

Group	Country	Aim
RAF (Red Army Faction)	Germany	Overthrow of the German state and the setting up of a revolutionary government.
BR (Red Brigades)	Italy	Overthrow of the Italian state; the setting up of a revolutionary government.
AD (Action Directe)	France	Overthrow of the French state and the setting up of a revolutionary government.
FLB (Breton Liberation Front)	France	Separation of Brittany from France.
ETA (Basque Separatists)	Spain	Full independence for the Basque region of Spain
IRA (Irish Republican Army)	United Kingdom	British withdrawal from Northern Ireland and reunification of Ireland
INLA (Irish National Liberation Army)	United Kingdom	British withdrawal from Northern Ireland and reunification of Ireland

Source 1   Examples of terrorist groups in western Europe since 1970.

The purpose of terrorism

A terrorist group usually has a political aim. This is to bring about a complete change in the country in which it operates. It might mean overthrowing the government or separating part of a country from the rest.

Terrorists think of themselves as 'political activists' and 'freedom fighters'. They destroy and kill as an 'act of war' and therefore do not consider themselves to be criminals. They feel that they cannot afford to let up, or be moderate in their actions. So they inflict a variety of actions against the society in which they live.

The example of the IRA

The Irish Republican Army is the military wing of the political party Sinn Fein, although Sinn Fein sometimes says there is no connection. It was set up during the First World War to force Britain to give Ireland independence. This did happen in 1921, but Northern Ireland remained part of the United Kingdom. The province was relatively quiet until the late 1960s, when the Catholic minority accused the Protestants of discriminating against them. Civil Rights demonstrations were held, which were followed by violence. In 1969 the British government sent in troops to restore order.

At this time the IRA came back into the picture, and the problem became one of terrorist violence as well as sectarian (religious) conflict. The aim of the IRA was to remove Northern Ireland from the United Kingdom, and to unite it with Eire. This is what the British government has so far consistently refused to do. As a result, the IRA increased its activities of bombing and shooting, mainly in Belfast and the border areas of Northern Ireland. In turn, violence was used, against Catholics, by Loyalist groups, who used terrorism to try to destroy the IRA and its hope of re-uniting Ireland.

Since the 1970s the IRA has also operated on the British mainland. It has killed a number of prominent people, including journalists and Members of Parliament. It attempted in 1984 to blow up the entire cabinet of the government at the Grand Hotel in Brighton, during the Conservative Party Conference. In 1991 it launched mortar shells into Downing Street as the cabinet was working there. It has also bombed pubs, railway stations, and buildings in the financial area of the City of London. A bomb which exploded in Warrington in March 1993 killed two boys, aged 3 and 12. There was such an outcry about this that the IRA felt it was necessary to justify itself.

Source 2

An IRA spokesman after the Warrington bombing, (*The Observer* newspaper, 28 March 1993).

There is an ongoing strategic objective which is to stretch the British police in terms of morale and resources. But we are not at war with the British population. From our point of view, there is nothing to be gained and a great deal to be lost from civilian casualties.

This has not prevented the IRA from making civilians their target in Britain and Northern Ireland in the past. Indeed, part of its goal is to bring the public in Britain to the point where it wants to be rid of Northern Ireland altogether.

Source 3

The aftermath of an IRA bomb explosion.

Actions to deal with terrorism

The problem facing the authorities

To some people, the solution is simple. The government should take the strongest possible measures to crush terrorism. This should involve the use of special powers, military force on a larger scale, and the return of the death sentence.

However, the problem is more complex than this. If the government introduces special powers it will undermine freedom for everyone. This is precisely what terrorists hope to achieve, so that the government will be strongly criticised by different groups within the population. If the government takes on total powers and makes full use of the army it will, of course, become a 'dictatorship'. Again, this would suit the terrorists.

The government therefore has to be very careful, in three ways:

1 It has to balance public security with individual freedom.

2 It has to take effective action against terrorists without increasing any sympathy for them.

3 It has to prevent the collapse of the public's morale to the point where they want to give in to terrorist demands.

Measures taken on the British mainland

Members of the public have had to experience inconvenience during attempts by the authorities to control IRA activities. These include many train cancellations and delays at mainline stations in Britain, and on the London Underground. Public locker facilities are no longer available, and there are fewer litter bins. There are also road checks at certain points, especially around the City of London financial area.

The main piece of government legislation was the Prevention of Terrorism Act (1974), which let the police keep terrorist suspects for up to seven days without charge. Three more Acts followed in the 1980s. The first Act was the Police and Criminal Evidence Act (1984), which reduced some of the restrictions on gathering evidence. The second Act was the Public Order Act (1986), which increased police powers in emergency situations. The third Act was the ban on terrorist broadcasting in 1989; this made it illegal to interview terrorists on television or to allow their spoken words to be heard 'on the air'.

These measures were, of course, very limited compared with those taken in Northern Ireland. There, for example, the Emergency Provisions Act of 1973 allowed for the courts to operate without juries, and gave the army powers of arrest and detention.

Source 4

A cartoon in *The Observer* newspaper, 28 March 1993.

Questions

1 When does 'protest' become 'terrorism'?

2 Terrorists argue that they should be treated as 'prisoners of war' if captured. The police and government argue that they are 'criminals'. What do you think?

3 Debate the statement 'To take tougher action against terrorists would play into their hands'.

4 Suggest arguments both for and against the return of capital punishment for terrorist killings. Which do you find more convincing? (See also pages 108–109.)

5 Has the British government succeeded in its balance between preserving public liberty and taking action against the IRA?

6 Explain the meaning of Source 4. Is it an accurate view, in the light of Source 1?

Changes in the police forces

Three major changes have taken place in the police forces since 1900. They have become fewer but larger, they have more specialist (or expert) groups within them, and they use more advanced equipment.

1 The number and size of forces

During the nineteenth century there were too many forces to be totally successful in the fight against crime. This was finally accepted between 1964 and 1974, when the total number of forces was reduced from 183 to 41. Many borough forces were joined with the county forces, and some counties with each other. This was part of the 1964 Police Act, and the process was completed by the 1974 Local Government Act. The result was a set of forces with new names like 'Thames Valley Police'. Counties were also grouped together in 1964 into Regional Crime Squads, to ensure close co-operation between the county constabularies.

2 Specialist groups

Although police forces have grown larger, they have tended to organise themselves into more specialist groups. These are intended to deal more effectively with specific types of problem. The Metropolitan Police Force (MPF) has led the way and the others have followed.

The first of these groups was the Flying Squad, set up by Scotland Yard in 1919. It was so named because of its use of cars to deal quickly with reports of criminal activity, especially robbery. This is now known as the Central Robbery Squad. In 1946, the Fraud Squad was established, followed in 1965 by the Special Patrol Group (SPG) to deal with inner-city disturbances. Other groups include the National Drugs Intelligence Unit and National Immigration Intelligence Unit (1972–3), the Diplomatic Protection Group, the Obscene Publications Squad, the Murder Squad, and the Bomb Squad.

3 Improvements in equipment

Scotland Yard also led the way in introducing new equipment. The MPF started to use radios in 1923, although these depended on the use of morse code. They were replaced by two-way radios for use in cars from 1934 onwards, and then during the 1960s personal radios were introduced for constables 'on the beat'. Other items now in regular use are metal detectors and infra-red equipment for detecting movement at night.

There have also been spectacular changes in forensic science. This involves using medical information to solve crimes. In the decade before the First World War, fingerprints were given a systematic classification (way of identifying each and every one). In 1935, a Metropolitan Police Laboratory was set up for the examination of any objects which might

Source 1

A typical police computer terminal.

offer clues. The most recent development, thought to be the biggest ever breakthrough in crime detection, is the use of 'genetic fingerprinting'. This means that a person can be identified from blood samples or other body fluids.

Police criminal hunts are based on building up information, or a profile, in order to match a crime to a suspect. Much of this material is of no use, but it can be sifted out by careful cross-checking. This means that large numbers of records have to be kept. Earlier in the century this was all very hard work, because it involved card indexes and traditional filing systems. A real breakthrough came with the computerisation of records from 1964 onwards. More material can be processed and found again later in a fraction of the time. Police in patrol cars now have access to computer operators in constabularies.

4 Use of firearms

The British police authorities have decided *not* to follow the example of the New York police, who give firearms (handguns) to all officers. On the other hand, training is provided in the use of firearms, and guns are used in certain cases. Originally police had access, when needed, to the .303 Lee Enfield rifle and the .38 Webley pistol. These have now been replaced by the L39A1 high-velocity rifle and the Smith and Wesson Model 10.

The role of the police in crime prevention

Units 7 and 8 included sections on measures against violence, theft, vandalism and rioting. How are the police involved in crime prevention? This is now seen as one of their major roles, and it takes two main forms.

1 Crime prevention officers and Neighbourhood Watch

Every force now has a number of crime prevention officers (CPOs), who advise on security and crime prevention. They speak at a variety of meetings, and visit people at work and students in schools when invited.

The Neighbourhood Watch scheme involves close co-operation between the police and members of the public. It was started in 1982 and spread to London, as an experiment by the Commissioner of the Metropolitan Police, Sir Kenneth Newman, in 1983. It was based on longer experiments in parts of the United States. Members of the community are asked to report suspicious behaviour to the police, who are then able to investigate immediately.

There is no doubt that such measures have led to a drop in some types of crime, especially burglary and theft. However, it could be argued that crime has increased in areas where such schemes are more difficult to operate.

2 Community policing

The idea behind this is the development of a close relationship and trust between the local community and the police. The Police and Criminal Evidence Act of 1984 stated that there should be consultation between the police and the local community in the form of committees. It is intended that, wherever possible, there should be 'Policing by consent'. Parents in the community should be encouraged to support the police by influencing their own children against crime, and by talking openly about any difficulties. One of the main problems, however, is that the police usually operate from cars, which make them more cut off from the community than the old

Source 2

A Neighbourhood Watch sticker.

'copper on the beat' had been. The use of cars has also increased the size of policing areas, so reducing the familiarity between the police and the community. Some forces, such as Lincolnshire, have tried to reverse this trend by using cars less.

During the 1980s the police faced a major crisis as many of Britain's inner cities erupted in violence. This, along with recommendations for police action, is dealt with on pages 99–101.

Attitudes to the police

Since 1960 much has been said and written about police methods; some attitudes are critical, others are favourable.

Uneasiness about police methods

There has always been concern about clashes between police and demonstrators, whether these involved CND or Vietnam protests in the 1960s, or industrial disputes like the miners' strike of 1984. In all of these the demonstrators claimed that the police behaved with unnecessary force.

During the 1970s the police were also accused of taking shortcuts in getting hold of evidence and confessions for terrorist offences like the Guildford and Birmingham bombings. The 'Guildford Four' and the 'Birmingham Six' were imprisoned on evidence put together by the police. This was later found to be faulty, and both groups were released after spending many years behind bars.

Police powers were also increased by the Police and Criminal Evidence Act of 1984, and the Public Order Act of 1986. The first Act gave police the power to stop and search people suspected of carrying stolen articles, or equipment for a burglary, or weapons. This has worried some members of the public.

Probably the largest problem concerning attitudes to the police has been in police relations with minority ethnics in Britain's inner city areas. This is discussed on pages 99–101.

The Police Complaints Authority (PCA) was set up in 1985 to deal with police inquiries into allegations (accusations) of corruption or unfair behaviour. There has, however, been some upset about the fact that the police investigate these problems themselves. The police response to this is to ask who else would have the training, experience and expertise to carry out such an investigation?

Continuing support for the police

Despite the problems of the 1970s and 1980s, the police still attract a great deal of public support, usually expressed in the popular press.

Source 3

The Sunday Mirror newspaper, 15 March 1986.

The Job, as the police call it, is getting tougher ... Many of them are bewildered by the conflicting demands that our changing society makes on them. In spite of that they show patience, tact and courage in conditions of extreme provocation. The overwhelming majority of Britain's policemen and policewomen are devoted to their duty, in spite of its difficulties. We acknowledge that dedication, and are proud of them.

To some extent public opinion has been affected by all the police-based dramas on British television, such as 'No Hiding Place', 'Dixon of Dock Green', 'Z-Cars', 'Softly-Softly', 'The Sweeney', 'The Bill' and many others.

The police also have the total support of the government.

Source 4

Home Office Minister, John Patten, in *The Guardian* newspaper, 4 September 1991.

I utterly condemn this mindless hooliganism and yobbery for which there can be no excuse. I hope all local people in the areas involved will back the police in the difficult job that has faced them.

Questions

1 Discuss in class the portrayal of the British police in television plays. How does it vary? Does it give the police a good or bad image?

2 What is the purpose of Source 2? Is it likely to work?

3 Debate the statement: 'A policeman's lot is not a happy one'.

4 'Policing has made huge progress since 1900.' Do you agree?

9.2 Changing attitudes to punishment

Capital punishment

The greatest change since 1900 in punishment has been the end of hanging. M.P.s in Westminster voted for the abolition of capital punishment for all crimes, except treason in war, in the Murder Act (Abolition of the Death Penalty) in 1965.

Since then there have been regular attempts to ask the question again, and bring back capital punishment for some types of murder. Debates took place in Parliament in 1969, 1972, 1973, 1974, 1975, 1979, 1982, 1983, 1986, and 1987. All of them produced the same result: a vote against changing the 1965 Act.

While most M.P.s have consistently shown one view, the majority of the general public have held another. Public opinion polls (surveys) since 1977 have shown that the percentage of public opinion favouring the return of hanging has sometimes gone over 80%, and has rarely been below 70%. The issue is therefore likely to remain a controversial one, as there are strong arguments for and against the return of capital punishment.

Source 1

Arguments *for* bringing back capital punishment.

1 It is a major deterrent. The threat of capital punishment would make intending robbers think twice before using, or even taking, a firearm.

2 Some forms of murder are so appalling that a special form of retribution is needed.

3 The victim's relatives deserve to have the shadow of the murderer removed from their lives. Capital punishment would therefore act as a form of restitution.

4 Bringing back capital punishment for acts of terrorism would show a tougher campaign by the authorities.

5 The United States has allowed the restoration of capital punishment; Britain would therefore not be the only western country to do so.

Source 2

Arguments *against* bringing back capital punishment.

1 It is barbaric for the state to take a life in cold blood: this would be 'judicial murder'.

2 It would be a step backwards to bring back a punishment which has already been abolished. Why not bring back flogging and the pillory as well?

3 It would not deter terrorists. The IRA and other groups might become martyrs for their cause, and there would also be more public sympathy for them.

4 There is always a chance of a miscarriage of justice, as in the case of the Guildford Four and the Birmingham Six.

5 There is always the chance of rehabilitation, even for the worst offenders.

6 Apart from the United States, no other western power has capital punishment. The United States has also had many controversies; one of these is that the vast majority of those executed are poor or black.

Source 3

The policy of the government on sentences for murder, according to the Home Secretary, Leon Brittan in 1983.

sadistic Inflicting pain for enjoyment.
custody Imprisonment.
gravity Seriousness.

Capital punishment has been replaced by life imprisonment, the punishment always given for murder. A minimum sentence can be specified by the judge and is nearly always backed by the Home Secretary.

Murderers of police or prison officers, terrorist murderers, sexual or sadistic murderers of children and murderers by firearm in the course of a robbery can normally expect to serve at least 20 years in custody; and there will be cases where the gravity of the offence requires a still longer period.

Country	Prisoners per 100,000 population
1 Austria	103
2 Turkey	100
3 Luxembourg	99
4 United Kingdom	96
5 France	89
6 Portugal	85
7 West Germany	84
8 Denmark	69
9 Belgium	69
10 Spain	67
11 Sweden	57
12 Italy	57
13 Ireland	54
14 Norway	50
15 Greece	40
16 Cyprus	38
17 Iceland	37
18 Netherlands	37
19 Malta	28

Imprisonment

The United Kingdom has a higher prison population per 100,000 population than any country in Europe, except for Austria, Turkey and Luxembourg. The length of sentences is also much longer than in most other countries in Europe, although not as long as in the United States.

The average number of prisoners has changed in Britain during the course of the twentieth century (see Source 5); with one exception the values show a steady increase.

Source 4

Britain's prison population compared with the rest of Europe, (1987).

Source 5

The average number of prisoners on any one day during some years in the twentieth century.

Date	Number
1900	17,800
1925	11,000
1950	20,000
1960	27,000
1967	35,000
1977	41,570
1987	48,425
1988	50,500

Who are these prisoners?

Source 6

Proportions of prisoners according to crimes committed, (1985).

Offence	Percentage of prisoners
Violence and sexual offences	19
Robbery	6
Burglary, theft, fraud, forgery, damage	41
Others	12
Remand (awaiting trial)	21

Imprisonment of young people

During the first decade of the twentieth century a special effort was made to give a separate form of punishment to young offenders. Between the ages of ten and seventeen, they were tried in separate courts. 'Borstals' were set up by the Prevention of Crime Act in 1908. These were junior prisons, with the emphasis on hard work and rehabilitation. Gradually, however, these were replaced by other forms of treatment for young offenders. These included detention centres, set up in 1948 with a maximum stay of four months.

Other institutions were called assessment and observation centres, and remand centres for those awaiting trial.

Problems in prisons

The ever-increasing prison population has led to serious overcrowding in Britain's prisons. Leeds prison, for example, is overpopulated by 95%, Bedford by 88%, Birmingham by 75%, Leicester by 72%, Manchester by 65%, and Hull by 59%. This means that prisoners have inadequate working and recreational facilities. They have to be kept in their cells for most of the day.

Riots have occurred on many recent occasions. In 1971, this happened in 41 prisons. There were serious disturbances in Wandsworth prison, London, in 1989, and in Strangeways prison, Manchester, in 1990.

Source 7

Prisoners sharing an over-crowded cell in Wormwood Scrubs.